KARY OBERBRUNNER

YOUR SECRET NAME

AN UNCOMMON QUEST TO STOP PRETENDING, SHED THE LABELS, AND DISCOVER YOUR TRUE IDENTITY

AUTHOR ACADEMY elite

Also by Kary Oberbrunner

ELIXIR PROJECT
DAY JOB TO DREAM JOB
THE DEEPER PATH
THE FINE LINE
CALLED
THE JOURNEY TOWARDS RELEVANCE

YOUR SECRET NAME © 2018 by Kary Oberbrunner.
All rights reserved.

Printed in the United States of America

Published by Author Academy Elite
P.O. Box 43, Powell, OH 43035
www.AuthorAcademyElite.com

All rights reserved. No part of this publication may be reproduced, stored in a retrieval system, or transmitted in any form or by any means—for example, electronic, photocopy, recording—without the prior written permission of the publisher. The only exception is brief quotations in printed reviews.

Library of Congress Cataloging 2018939582

Softcover: 978-1-64085-265-5
Hardcover: 978-1-64085-266-2
Audiobook: 978-1-64085-267-9

Available in hardcover, softcover, e-book, and audiobook

All Scripture quotations, unless otherwise indicated, are taken from the Holy Bible, *New International Version*®, *NIV*®. Copyright © 1973, 1978, 1984 by Biblica, Inc.™ Used by permission of Zondervan. All rights reserved worldwide.

Scripture quotations marked TNIV are taken from the Holy Bible, *Today's New International Version*™. *TNIV*®. Copyright © 2001, 2005 by Biblica, Inc.™ Used by permission of Zondervan. All rights reserved worldwide.

Scripture quotations marked NASB are taken from the *New American Standard Bible*®, Copyright © 1960, 1962, 1963, 1968, 1971, 1972, 1973, 1975, 1977, 1995 by The Lockman Foundation. Used by permission.

Any Internet addresses (websites, blogs, etc.) and telephone numbers printed in this book are offered as a resource. They are not intended in any way to be or imply an endorsement by Author Academy Elite, nor does Author Academy Elite vouch for the content of these sites and numbers for the life of this book.

*For Linda Outka
You embody Breakthrough Solutions.*

Thanks for taking a chance on me as your coach and spreading the Secret Name message.

CONTENTS

Foreword xi
A Note to the Reader. xiii
Introduction: The Gentle Whisper. 1

PART 1: WHAT'S IN A NAME?

1. A World Without Names. 9
2. The Statue Maker 19
3. The Name Game. 26

PART 2: ACCEPTING THE PRESENT

4. Puppets and Pawns 37
5. Imposter Syndrome. 46
6. Till We Have Names 56
7. Three Heartbreaks. 66

PART 3: EMBRACING THE FUTURE

8. Grace Interrupted 77
9. Mirrors Tell Half-Truths 83

YOUR SECRET NAME

10. Packing Your Suitcase 91
11. In the Camp of Angels. 96

PART 4: YOUR SECRET NAME

12. Pushing Through the Past 107
13. The Divine Wound 114
14. The White Stone 122
15. Sacred Spaces 129
Epilogue: Firsts and Lasts 142

APPENDICIES

1. Additional Insight on Your Secret Name 145
2. The ABCs of your Identity. 153
3. Discussion Points 155
4. Notes 163

Acknowledgments. 167
About the Author 169
About the Publisher 171
About Igniting Souls 173
Your Next Steps with Your Secret Name. 175

*And now we're grown-up orphans
That never knew their names.*
—"Name," Goo Goo Dolls

FOREWORD

We live a highlight-reel world. We don't sit through games as much as we catch the top 10. More people watch movie trailers than actually watch movies. We fall in love with the product, but we forget about the process.

This reminds me of a story about my friend Kevin. He has the sharpest wit of anyone I know.

When he was sixteen, he was working at a grocery store, mopping in the vegetable aisle. An older woman came up and said, "I would like to have half a head of lettuce." He said, "Ma'am, I don't know about that… I'll have to go and ask my supervisor."

Kevin went to the back of the store and found his manager. He said, "This crazy old woman just walked up into the vegetable section and said that she wanted half a head of lettuce."

Kevin didn't know that the woman had followed him at a distance and had caught up just in time to hear the end of his last sentence. As Kevin was finishing his statement, he looked over his shoulder and noticed her standing there. He immediately said, "And this beautiful woman right here said that she would take the other half."

Many of us only want half a head of lettuce. We only want the success half, even though we know certain disciplines are necessary to get it. We know the right things to do—our problem is getting them done. We don't have a truth problem.

We have a training problem. If all we needed were truth, the word "diet" wouldn't exist.

Let me say it another way, this time stronger: *We want the product without the process.*

We all desire great relationships. However, it's a big investment to cultivate them. We want successful careers, super kids (if we have kids), and healthy spiritual lives. We wish the magic spirit fairy would come and sprinkle holy dust on us without any rearranging on our part.

But true transformation requires something deeper. I'm convinced now more than ever that step one is identifying our identity.

We must know who we are in relation to eternity, legacy, and even society.

In *Your Secret Name,* Kary helps us discover the other half, the part we don't know. His book isn't a formula but a mission and a process that leads to a real product. The truth is there's no magic dust. You must know who you truly are, and the only way to get there is through the application of some basic principles.

Discovering your identity is an adventure. It's also a requirement for those who want to live a life of purpose, leave a legacy worth following, and look forward to a secure eternity. We can all achieve this, but we cannot skip the process.

I'm incredibly grateful for my friendship with Kary Oberbrunner. He treats people with dignity and lives with integrity, and I know you can trust him.

Get ready to discover who God created you to be. I know you'll never look at yourself, God, or life the same way again.

Dean Fulks
Author of *Your Next 30 Days,*
Lead Pastor at Life Point Church

A NOTE TO THE READER

My name is Kary, and I want to thank you for investing your energy in this book. I encourage you not to skip this brief note. It will make more sense in a moment.

We both know you could be doing a million other things with your time. Instead, you've chosen to explore the concept of *Your Secret Name*. For this reason, I believe you'll be richly rewarded, but perhaps not in the way you might think.

Here's what I mean.

This message has the power to change the way you see yourself and the world. I know this because of the testimonies of others—thousands of others. This book has now lived and breathed for nearly ten years. It's traveled the world, and it's found its way into the hearts and minds of young and old alike.

I can't take a single ounce of credit or blame for anything this book births in you. Quite frankly, I don't even remember writing it. I just reread the manuscript for the first time in nearly a decade, and to put it bluntly, it was one of the strangest experiences I've ever had.

For starters, I didn't recognize the author. I say that without a shred of hyperbole. Ernest Hemingway is often credited with the saying "There is nothing to writing. All you do is sit down at a typewriter and bleed." He's correct—except for the typewriter part because I used a computer.

When I wrote *Your Secret Name*, I bled—and it was a whole bunch of blood too. Back in 2009, I was a full-time pastor, and I had never shared about my past in a public way. I knew doing so could be dangerous. I wondered if I'd lose my job or my friends or my reputation.

In a way, I lost all three and much more. But again, not as you might think. Thankfully, the church where I worked supported *Your Secret Name*, and me for that matter. I'll forever be grateful for that.

But I quickly learned that the message itself was dangerous. Once it got out, I was uninvited to events. Other people wrote blog posts condemning my view of God and life. One leader told his pastor he'd boycott an event if I came and spoke at his church. I spoke anyway. And that man was true to his word. He never showed up.

I realized that some people aren't *ready* for the truth. Still others don't want to *hear* the truth. And only a few brave souls are willing to *pursue* the truth.

Although I often hear stories of transformation resulting from *Your Secret Name*, I believe the life that changed the most was my own. This is why I can honestly say that I don't recognize the thirty-two-year-old kid who wrote the book.

Now I'm in my forties. I have less hair—or, more accurately, no hair at all. But it was this book that helped me take the first step in becoming a soul on fire. It helped me discover who God created me to be.

When I finished *writing Your Secret Name*, I knew I needed to start *living* my Secret Name. A couple of years after Zondervan published the book, I left my role as a pastor. Although I still loved the church, I knew I needed to become an entrepreneur to do my own gig and manifest all that was in my heart.

Today, I ignite souls full-time, often in the business context.

Since discovering my Secret Name, I haven't done well with boxes, categories, or labels. Maybe that's why I feel compelled to warn you. This book has the potential to reshape your beliefs about God, life, and even yourself. But only if you let it.

A NOTE TO THE READER

If I were to write this book for the first time today, it would be completely different. That's the weird thing about being an author. A book is a snapshot of who you are at a moment in time. When you change, so does the way you think and the way you write.

For this reason, I tried to expand and update as little as possible. I wanted to keep the integrity of the message and only polish when necessary. I'm grateful that Zondervan reverted the rights to me. They didn't have to, but they chose to because of the work we're still doing around *Your Secret Name*.

Thousands of people are still finding their Secret Names. Many of them are going beyond the book and into the course, the events, and the global team of speakers, coaches, and trainers. They're taking the message into schools, churches, organizations, and anywhere else people need freedom.

Welcome to *Your Secret Name*—an uncommon quest to stop pretending, shed the labels, and discover your true identity. I can't wait for you to find out what awaits you on the other side.

Talk soon. And remember: I believe in you.

—Kary

Introduction
The Gentle Whisper

Tomorrow night I could change my little girl's future forever—and strangely, she isn't even born yet.

On our "date night"—an infrequent event for two parents with two other children under the age of four—my wife, Kelly, and I will go to a local bookstore, sit down with a stack of books, and participate in a ritual as old as humanity itself.

We're going to pick out a name for a child we've never met. At least that's the plan.

With only eight weeks left in the pregnancy, we can't afford to stall. Unfortunately, we've been having the same date night for the last several months, and we're no closer to choosing a name. When we come home, our babysitter can tell with one glance at our dejected faces that we're going to need her services again, and sooner than any of us thought.

Naming our first two kids posed a few obstacles, but at the present moment, this third one has us caught in a cruel headlock and almost ready to tap out. Until we settle on a name we're gridlocked, unable to move an inch in any other area of our fast-paced lives.

As a guy, coming home without a name feels similar to returning from a hunt without a kill—or maybe from the hardware store without that critical part (although admittedly

I don't often venture into the realm of home improvement). In any case, my inability to score the right name undermines any hope of fulfilling the "masculine stereotype" of a problem solver.

Kelly doesn't feel any better.

She paces the house at all hours of the night, penciling possibilities that seem impossible when examined in the light of day. Somehow, both of us feel beaten by this task, and every day that we fail to come up with a name is another day closer to our daughter's birth.

At some point in history, we humans decided assigning names in infancy was a good idea. Our parents got suckered into the same strategy because they had the same pattern modeled to them.

The tradition isn't all bad, as there are some benefits to bestowing names early on. No one wants to be referred to as "girl" or "hey you" for the bulk of their childhood. Yet our need for names bleeds much deeper than birth certificates on official papers and lingers much longer than the echo from the server's voice at Panera Bread announcing that our "Pick Two" soup and salad combo is ready to be picked up at the counter.

The truth is, every single person who's breathing in this same air on planet Earth is also caught up in the same age-old Name Game. And as long as we're stuck in the Name Game—the unsuccessful cycle of trying to discover our true identity independently of God—rest assured, we'll never win.

On the contrary, we'll always be swept away with a dose of angst that often feels as colossal as planet Earth.

Think I'm exaggerating? Let me ask then:

- Are you completely secure in understanding who you are?
- Are you confident you know your true identity?

- Are you fully resolved concerning certain monumental issues, like discerning your purpose, calling, and lot in this life?

If not, don't feel discouraged. Instead, realize these feelings are both normal and natural. God planted these questions deep inside your soul in order that you'd eventually discover the path that leads to him. Or, more accurate, so that you'd reach the end of yourself and then finally be ready to experience the beginning of him. The Bible tells us: "He has made everything beautiful in its time. He has also set eternity in the human heart."

Essentially, we're all homesick for a place we've never been. And so we live as nomads, groping toward a destination we can't quite define. As creatures we fumble along, hoping to find our way back to the One who made us—believing that as we discover who *we* truly are, we also discover a portion of who *he* truly is.

Anthropologists agree with this phenomenon, at least in part. They understand uncertainty infects every person in every culture and that each one of us desperately desires the answer to the most basic question:

"WHO AM I?"

These three simple words hijack our brains at an early age, clutching onto our core, nagging us wherever we go. Children seek to answer this question in playtime by assigning titles like Mommy or Daddy when playing house or labels like cops and robbers when playing bank heist.

Adults seek to answer this question with more sophisticated strategies. Some of us climb our way up the corporate ladder, plowing through perpetual promotions. While others of us maintain our reputation of trendy and hip by sporting the latest gadgets and trinkets. In the checkout line at the mall, we buy the lie that a new jacket or pair of shoes will somehow dispel the hurt we feel in our hearts. But the excitement soon fades, and our souls are once again exposed as naked and needy.

We incorrectly assume that names given by other people or other things will somehow scratch our identity itch.

Yet Birth Names (the names assigned to us when we *arrive* in this world) and Given Names (the positive and negative titles we inherit while *walking* in this world) were never hardwired to alleviate the tension.

On the contrary, they only fuel it, creating more space between our true identity and us.

And so many of us spend a lifetime running from our Given Names, exchanging our best years, hoping to escape these false words that reach out and long to define us. But transcending these titles is no simple task.

Slowly over time, these labels become part of our permanent wardrobe. And as we wear them, we end up settling for so much less than we were born to be.

We'd do well to swallow the truth—that such names are never enough. Neither our Birth Name nor our Given Names expel the ache or satisfy our souls. None serve as a substitute for our Secret Name.

Secret Name?

That probably sounds a bit strange, or at a minimum, unfamiliar.

But that's only because our vocabulary doesn't often venture into epic realms, realms of destiny and legacy. Instead, we frequently prefer trivial topics, like other people's attempts at dieting, our favorite college team's road to the championship, or our friend's most recent status update on the latest social networking site. But let's not be too hard on ourselves. We're not shallow people. Rather, we've just gotten used to relating on levels that avoid soul issues.

For a thousand reasons, it's much easier this way.

Good thing God has much more in mind. He wants to grant you a new name—a Secret Name, in fact—but you can only start embracing your future name when you stop running from your present ones.

THE GENTLE WHISPER

You must accept who you are in order to discover who you were created to be.

———⊸⊷⊶⊷⊸———

This book is about giving up the Name Game. It's about putting an end to chasing the false names that offer only a hollow promise. It's about finally encountering your Secret Name, drinking it down, and allowing it to ooze into every quadrant of your life the ones you can see—and those you can't.

As you might have guessed, discovering your Secret Name isn't a painless process. And they aren't bestowed to the masses either, only unto the remnant courageous enough to deal with their junk.

The first step is to turn down the noise a few notches. The world perpetually shouts and screams, seeking to brand you.

Your true name—your Secret Name—is granted only by the One who knew you before you were born.

In all this, remember, the Father doesn't speak with a loud voice, but most often with a gentle whisper. Tragically, we rarely stay quiet long enough to hear him.

Then a great and powerful wind tore the mountains apart and shattered the rocks before the Lord, but the Lord was not in the wind. After the wind there was an earthquake, but the Lord was not in the earthquake. After the earthquake came a fire, but the Lord was not in the fire. And after the fire came a gentle whisper.

1 Kings 19:11–12

PART ONE

What's in a Name?

*A bad wound may heal,
but a bad name will kill.*

—Scottish proverb

1
A WORLD WITHOUT NAMES

You may be surprised to learn that I share a bond with the cool cat who hosted the hit game show *Wheel of Fortune*—a bond so strong that you might say our destinies are intertwined forever.

Pat Sajack and I both have a girl's name.

Don't laugh.

Growing up with a girl's name wasn't easy. More than once I remember the mean kids circling me, wickedly chanting, "Kary has a girl's name. Kary has a girl's name."

I remember I got a piece of mail addressed to *Ms.* Kary Oberbrunner. It was an invitation to an all-girls summer cheerleading camp. Good thing my friends never saw that brochure. Come to think of it, upon opening it, I burned it—promptly.

Such acts of naming slowly ate away my security, eroding my confidence like a constant drip of water over time erodes a menacing solid block of concrete.

Eventually I reached a breaking point.

I had to stop the pain, and I decided building myself up physically would solve the problem. Television convinced me that putting on some serious muscle would silence the malicious taunts. Strength worked for Mr. T and the A-Team, and I believed it just might work for me too.

Since steroids are hard to come by in the first grade, I settled for a much faster strategy. One morning, while in my bedroom getting ready for school, I stuffed my tiny navy blue sweater full of socks. I thought a dozen balled-up socks placed strategically in my sleeves and chest area would add an edge to my image and give me a new name, perhaps Spike or Rock. I walked into class, sweater bulging with fake muscles. The kids circled me as usual, but instead of calling me names, they looked on with strange curiosity.

I was thrilled. My brilliant plan was giving me the empowerment I craved—until one of my "muscles" fell out of my sweater and onto the floor.

I received a new name that day—IDIOT.

The school year inched by slowly that year. I longed for summer afternoons where my cousins and I were the kings of the woods behind their house—where we would invent our own names for each other, names consistent with our other favorite TV shows, old shows, like the *Dukes of Hazzard*, *MacGyver*, and the *Greatest American Hero*, popularized by its theme song "Believe It or Not."

Unfortunately for us, there was nothing believable about our make-believe playtime, and each school year jolted us back to reality. My classmates knew nothing about the clever aliases my cousins and I assigned each other.

Thankfully, not everyone at my school was cruel.

At recess one day, a particular girl decided she'd seen enough of my verbal beatings and decided to oppose the mean kids. "Stop making fun of Kary," she said.

"Why should we? He has a girl's name," one particular bully pointed out reasonably.

"So?" my defender shot back, searching for some type of logical defense.

"There're plenty of cool guys with girl's names."

"Oh yeah? Like who?" The bully wasn't about to back down.

We all wondered if she'd manage a rebuttal. With my self-esteem on the line, I desperately prayed she would.

"Pat Sajack," she blurted out. "He's cool, and Pat's *definitely* a girl's name."

Pat Sajack? I thought. *I guess he's cool.* Maybe I was hoping for someone a little . . . taller?

Although we humans tend to fixate on names, at one point in history, this simply wasn't the case. Rewind time way back to the beginning when a much different world existed—specifically, a world without names. The first two chapters of Genesis refer to the first two people as man/woman, male/female, and man/wife. These individuals were identified for what they were (gender and species), not for who they were (personal names).

Remarkably, an environment devoid of sin also meant an environment devoid of human names.[1] Perhaps difficult to imagine, but names were simply unnecessary in those days. Since the original man and woman knew who God was, they also knew who they were—an inescapable by-product. And so the insatiable question presently seared into our brains—Who am I?—didn't exist because separation from God didn't exist. The core question of identity found its idyllic resolution within a pure relationship with the Father.

Prior to the fall, detailed in chapter three of Genesis, the first two people experienced perfect harmony with their Creator. They walked and talked with God intimately and frequently. Names existed in the garden of Eden, but only names that described *what* beings were, not *who* these beings were.

God placed the responsibility on man to name the lower order, thereby fulfilling his original command to "Be fruitful and increase in number; fill the earth and subdue it. Rule over the fish of the sea and the birds of the air and over every living creature that moves on the ground." According to God's will, the man obediently assigned names to all of the animals and birds:

> *Now the Lord God had formed out of the ground all the beasts of the field and all the birds of the air. He brought them to the man to see what he would name them; and whatever the man called each living creature, that was its name. So the man gave names to all the livestock, the birds of the air and all the beasts of the field.*
>
> Genesis 2:19–20

Yet, for man and woman at this time, there was no need for names—that is until sin emerged and ripped them away from God. A fractured relationship *with* God meant a fractured understanding *of* God as well as a fractured understanding of themselves— also an inescapable by-product. By losing their grasp of who God was, they also lost their grasp of who they were. The damage now done and the ground now cursed, the man's next response proved both chilling and revealing.

Guess what he did immediately.

Adam names his wife—Eve.

God never told him to name her. Only a chapter before, this act of naming, commanded by God himself, was reserved for Adam to bestow names upon animals, not fellow human beings. Pulling back the layers, we see how sin infects a person, even within the first few minutes of contracting the fatal disease.

By naming his wife, Adam attempted ineffectively to solve a riddle well above his pay grade. No other human can answer for us our deepest question of identity.

Sin causes us to treat other people as less than human— more specifically, like animals. And sin seductively whispers the lie that we'll find our true identity by naming others or by receiving names from other people.

A WORLD WITHOUT NAMES

Deception now feeding our souls, the truth is that an inaccurate view of God yields an inaccurate view of ourselves—a dilemma we often rush to remedy. But factor God out of the equation and we're left only with using our own efforts to score a new identity, a trend found just a few chapters later in Genesis.

Humankind tried to combine its collective energy in an attempt to provide an answer to the age-old, sin-induced question: Who am I? This mass of humanity slaved away and built the Tower of Babel for no other reason than to forge a new name. They hoped that by carving out stone, they'd somehow carve out their Secret Name too.

> *"Then they said, 'Come, let us build ourselves a city, with a tower that reaches to the heavens, so that we may make a name for ourselves and not be scattered over the face of the whole earth.'"*
>
> Genesis 11:4

Fast-forward and the story is still being retold. We're caught up in the same Name Game, carving out new names, trying to satisfy the same ache. You'd think after all this time we would've learned idyllic resolution is *still* only found within a pure relationship with the Father.

But we haven't learned, and so we enter this war-torn world with a few strikes against us. Unfortunately, we arrive with a Birth Name.

Birth Names aren't the enemy, but they certainly aren't a friend either. They don't offer any clarity regarding the question—Who am I?—if that's what you're wondering. Birth Names offer different levels of insight, depending on where you're from, but they can never replace the need for discovering our Secret Name.

Many cultures bestow Birth Names based on their meaning, but Westerners tend to choose ones predominantly based on the way they roll off the tongue.

YOUR SECRET NAME

We may pick a name because it's popular or because someone we admire holds the name. Perhaps a few expectant parents even settle on a name based on its etymology. But for the vast majority, choosing a Birth Name is almost totally dependent on personal preference.

Not so for hundreds of other cultures around the world, including Africans, Arabs, and East Indians. For many of these cultures, a name describes a person, often referring to his or her physical characteristics.

Customs expert James M. Freeman explains:

> *Thus a certain Abyssinian was named Omazena, because of a wart on his hand; an Arab boy was called Duman, because he was born before the gate of Bab-el-Duma at Damascus. Among the Hindoos we find Ani Muttoo, the precious pearl; Pun Amma, the golden lady; Chinny Tamby, the little friend. Among the Native American Indians we have Kosh-kin-ke-kait, the cut-off arm; Wah-ge-kaut, crooked legs; Wau-zhe-gaw-maish-kum, he that walks along the shore.*[2]

For such people groups, one's Birth Name marks a person for life, and changing it is out of the question.

Within the biblical tradition, naming proved an even weightier undertaking. For these cultures, a particular name often carried a prophetic commentary. Your Birth Name shaped how you acted and who you became, functioning as a window into your behavior and temperament. This pattern begins in the first few pages of Genesis, the first book of the Bible. When Eve gives birth to her first child, a son, she says, "With the help of the Lord I have brought forth a man."

Eve named him Cain, meaning "acquisition" or "possession." The name *Cain* is related to the Hebrew verb *I acquired*. Some scholars feel that Eve's name choice represented her belief that Cain would fulfill God's prophetic statement concerning the promised seed that would come from her.[3]

Eve named her second son Abel, which means "breath," "vapor," or "vanity" and seems to relate to shortness of life spoken of much later in the Scriptures.[4] We observe that jealousy *possessed* Cain as he observed God's favor for Abel's sacrifice rather than his. Cain wished he could *acquire* God's favor, so he cut his brother's life short.

With Abel dead and Cain disqualified (murder tends to have that effect), "God gave Adam and Eve another son— Seth—which means 'the appointed, the substitute' (taking Abel's place)."[5]

As the centuries rolled on, the plot thickened. God has always been calling a people out for himself—in the Old Testament predominantly the Israelites, and in the New Testament predominantly the church. The Israelites originated from Jacob, the younger son of Isaac, the promised son of Abraham, who was the father of many nations and the recipient of God's unconditional covenant.

Echoing the choices of Cain and Abel, the younger of the twins (Jacob) shrewdly stole the birthright of the older brother (Esau) with a covert act of deception. Jacob invited Esau to exchange his inheritance for a bowl of stew. At the end of the meal deal, Esau might have had a full stomach, but most certainly he also had an empty soul.

Jacob received his Birth Name, meaning "deceiver" and "heel grabber," because he exited the womb clutching his twin brother's heel. Labeled a "schemer" and "one who undermines," Jacob lived up to his name repeatedly at the expense of his brother Esau.

Jacob needed transformation and, more than that, he needed a new name— especially if God would build his chosen people through Jacob's lineage. How could God name his people after a patriarch who habitually manipulated and swindled others through scheming?

As if being called a "deceiver" wasn't bad enough, Jacob had to deal with the shameful connotations that clung to any name associated with the "heel." In the Old Testament, God linked Satan himself to the first reference to the heel, prophesying that the evil Serpent would one day bruise the heel of Eve's future offspring.[6]

"Heel" received some additional poor marks in the New Testament. In one of history's darkest moments, on the threshold of Judas's betrayal, Jesus identified the turncoat disciple as the one who "lifted up his heel against me."

Jacob, the future father of the twelve tribes of Israel, spent a lifetime running from both his Birth Name and his Given Names. If Jacob hoped to inherit his divine destiny, he needed an entirely new identity.

He needed to learn his Secret Name.

Chances are that somewhere along the way, you've been tagged with a Given Name[7] that you're not too crazy about:

ORPHAN	HEALTHY	STUTTERER
RICH	AGNOSTIC	DEPRESSED
POWERLESS	VENGEFUL	UNPROTECTED
WEAK	BRILLIANT	ATHLETE
LOST	COMMON	SINNER
UNCREATIVE	TRAPPED	HANDICAPPED
MISTAKE	OVERWHELMED	INCAPACITATED
ACCIDENT	TIRED	INVALID
UGLY	VICTIM	DISABLED
BATTERED	REJECTED	BORED
EXHAUSTED	UNSEEN	BURDENED
FATHERLESS	INVISIBLE	COCKY
EXPOSED	FORGOTTEN	DESPAIRING
FAITHLESS	ABANDONED	IGNORANT
UNWANTED	RUSHED	IDIOT
ARROGANT	HASTY	FOOLISH

A WORLD WITHOUT NAMES

UNTOUCHABLE	PLAIN	SPINELESS
SELF-RELIANT	SLUT	FEARFUL
UNABLE	SIMPLE	WIMP
SUCCESSFUL	DISPOSABLE	BANKRUPT
UNSURE	DOWNCAST	FRIENDLESS
UNSTABLE	SOMBER	DAMNED
HOSTAGE	MELANCHOLY	CURSED
ABDUCTED	LEGALISTIC	UNLUCKY
ENSLAVED	TAINTED	ACCURSED
CAPTIVE	TRAMP	CLUMSY
POOR	IMPURE	AWKWARD
HOMELESS	DIRTY	FAT
BUM	DEFENSELESS	ANOREXIC
GIFTED	OPPRESSED	CUTTER
NEEDY	SINGLE	SELF-INJURER
FAILURE	DISTURBED	LAZY
DISCONTENTED	TROUBLED	BLAH
DISTRAUGHT	CRIMINAL	FREELOADER
SICK	GUILTY	SUICIDAL
UNHEALTHY	ESTRANGED	USED
DISEASED	BANISHED	PERPETRATOR
VIOLENT	MISFIT	MOLESTER
WHORE	COLD	UNBALANCED
TENSE	CALLOUSED	STRESSED
ALONE	IMPATIENT	OFFENSIVE
JUDGED	UNAPPRECIATED	UNPRODUCTIVE
MISJUDGED	OUTCAST	WASTEFUL
POPULAR	UNLOVED	LIAR
DIVORCED	RELIGIOUS	DECEPTIVE
UNSKILLED	FAMISHED	UNCERTAIN
INCAPABLE	UNFULFILLED	AVERAGE
UNFAITHFUL	INDECISIVE	UNIMPRESSIVE
ADDICT	BROKEN	
HELPLESS	LOSER	

Most of us spend a lifetime running from these Given Names, wasting our best years trying to escape words that trap and define us. But transcending these terms isn't a simple task.

God desires a different outcome. He has a Secret Name for each one of his children, and he whispers to all those who will listen, "He who has an ear, let him hear what the Spirit says to the churches. To him who overcomes, to him I will give *some* of the hidden manna, and I will give him a white stone, and a new name written on the stone which no one knows but he who receives it" (Revelation 2:17 NASB).

For each of us, the pretending will stop—either in this life or the next. But only a few of us choose to learn our Secret Name this side of eternity. The rest of us have gotten so used to the bondage, we remain content only knowing our Given Names.

Jacob might never have learned his Secret Name either, but during his exile in which he ran from his vengeful brother, he had a dream. Through this dream, God showed Jacob a different way and a different world, and when he awoke from his dream, he thought, "Surely the Lord is in this place, and I was not aware of it."

Jacob had no idea that God planned to build a nation through him. He couldn't imagine the lands he would one day inherit or fathom that the blood flowing through his veins would, centuries later, animate David and Solomon. He couldn't foresee Jesus, the Promised Redeemer, would descend from his son Judah.

But before any of this could happen, Jacob needed to discover his Secret Name. That would make all the difference.

You too need to be awakened by God's whisper in a dream because, most likely, you have no idea of all the wonderful plans God wants to lavish upon you.

So are you ready to discover your Secret Name?

Learning it will make all the difference.

I know it did for me.

2
THE STATUE MAKER

At a young age, my brother, two sisters, and I realized our parents weren't in the running to win the "First Out of Church on Sunday Morning" award.

Wondering if Jesus would come back to earth sooner than our parents would emerge through the exit door, we decided to innovate. In order to survive the boredom, we created a unique game called "statue maker."

Chock full of imagination, our game boasted a multiplicity of positions.

Although all of us desired a particular role, only one lucky person landed the coveted "statue maker." The rest of us became statues—except for the unfortunate kid tapped to be the "shopper."

In the pregame phase, the statue maker spun her statues one at a time.

Round and round, round and round, and when released, the statues froze their poses. Those of us challenged by gravity, usually the younger ones, tended to fall instantly to the ground. Others, mostly older kids, stumbled and teetered, trying to regain balance, to everyone's amusement. Each statue froze in a different shape—some on all fours, others with both arms extended upward, and others even flat on their backs.

However a statue emerged from the statue maker's spin, he or she had to remain fixed in *that* pose. If the shopper caught any statues moving prematurely, they were immediately disqualified, even before the game started.

Still in the pregame phase, each of us statues needed to receive one critical piece of information—our secret name.

LION

LLAMA

BALLERINA

BASKETBALL PLAYER

Our secret names varied, as did our poses, yet we all received our identities in the same manner—with a gentle whisper.

The statue maker studied our frozen forms, looking for the essence of what was locked inside, waiting to come to life. She'd confront that essence and cultivate it by granting each of us a new name. Upon hearing her whisper, our hearts raced as did our minds as we began to calculate how to best embody our new identity.

With secret names fully distributed the game officially began.

At that point, the shopper entered the imaginary store and asked to see the statue maker's statues. Expectancy crackled in the air as the statues mentally rehearsed the moves required of them upon their awakening—from roars to leaps to twirls.

Although currently comatose lumps of clay, we'd soon come to life.

Walking by us, one at a time, the shopper examined our awkward and sometimes downright silly poses. If he wanted to find out more about a particular statue, he'd touch the statue on the head, giving it permission to come alive. With that touch, the statue's eyes opened, it sprang to life, and the gate of creativity swung open to release the flood. Leaping and lunging, jumping and crawling, we embraced our new identity with fearless fervor. Finally unleashed, we embodied artistry, our imagination now our only boundary.

One at a time, we continued our dance until the shopper's hand touched us on the head again, thus refreezing us. Although the shopper's goal was to discover our secret names, the goal of each statue was equally clear. We wanted our dance so believable that the shopper risked his guess on our identity. If, through our passionate portrayal, a statue emerged worthy of *that* risk, and assuming the shopper guessed our secret name correctly, the respective statue became the coveted statue maker in the next round.

Our game was a dance of self-discovery and self-revelation. Thinking back to my childhood, I'm glad we had the chattiest parents in the church.

While playing statue maker, were we dancing near the divine?

As children, were we tiptoeing near something deeper that as adults we often fail to recognize?

One time Jesus addressed some adults fighting over whose name was the best and over who was the greatest in the kingdom. He said, "I tell you the truth, unless you change and become like little children, you will never enter the kingdom of heaven."

As I have come to see it now, the Statue Maker is God. He designs us, shapes us, and names us in love.

This creation process is mysterious, at times even painful. For many of us, this pain is deep and, in some cases, unspeakable. But understand that God sees and feels this pain. He's not a cosmic watchmaker, uncaring and uninvolved, winding up the world and then retreating to more exciting endeavors. Believing that God cruelly uses us as pawns is simply a lie some of us tell ourselves in order to avoid more pain.

How come?

It's far less painful to pretend that God doesn't care—that he's detached and distant and eternally discontent—than to believe that God is cognizant of and concerned with every detail of our lives. We often prefer a distant God. Such thinking is safer and less complicated. God is in heaven and we're on earth. He lives his life and we live ours. As the first man and woman discovered in Eden, there's comfort in hiding from God.

After all, when he finds us hiding, he'll discover that we're naked. Better to pretend that we've got everything under control than to admit our own shame, frailty, and need.

But if we're honest, we sometimes wonder: If God is powerful, why doesn't he stop the pain? Or, if he allows pain despite his power, doesn't that prove he's cruel? We begin to question whether we can trust God. And if the answer is no, if we can't trust him, then we don't have a chance of loving him.

Fear him?

Maybe.

But never love him?

Living in fear, some of us choose *rebellion*. We think it's less painful to pretend that God doesn't exist, and so we make ourselves god. We manipulate people so we can obtain our most coveted commodity: control. With people and possessions in our back pocket, we buy the illusion of a pain-free existence.

Living in fear, others of us choose *religion*. We make God into something he's not. We try to manipulate and control this false god with good works to obtain our most coveted commodity: also control. With strict obedience to rules and rituals, we believe our god is somehow appeased and our good behavior will spare us from a pain-filled existence.

Although both paths are dressed up a bit differently, they lead to the same lonely place—isolation.

We know this.

We feel this and we taste this.

Like lost ships drifting in the ocean, we inherently know we're meant for a destination. Only this particular destination isn't a place, but rather a Person—the Statue Maker, to be exact.

Whether you believe in God or not, he believes in you. He fashions each of us according to his likeness. And even though we all have the divine spark within us, most of us never acknowledge this divine thought. As in my childhood game, we try to *act* our part before we *know* our part.

But without first knowing who we are—without hearing our Secret Name whispered by the Statue Maker—we have no other choice than to exist as unidentified individuals, privy only to whatever names the world wants to assign to us.

Consider the nearest high school.

Many teens are ruthless. They classify and identify, categorize and patronize, ensuring that everyone knows where he or she fits in the food chain. Cliques set themselves up as judge and jury, deciding which teen to emulate and which one to regurgitate.

But the plot doesn't change much as we age. Just the other day, I had breakfast with a successful lawyer in his sixties. While discussing the premise of this book, he shared the nickname his father pegged him with. Whether his father meant it or not, calling his clumsy son "Moose" proved to have far-reaching effects. To this day, in moments of living life on autopilot, he's still trying to shed this Given Name, just like the rest of us.

Names cut deep and stick with us our whole life. We can't measure how much we compensate or overcompensate for the voices set on repeat within our subconscious. Much of what we do is a reaction to these labels. It's why we

- vow to prove them wrong.

- never take a risk.

- get that surgery.
- buy that item.
- take that job.
- don't speak up.
- wake up early.
- stay up late.
- look at that.
- refuse to eat this.

Given Names shape us. They make us, and they can even break us.

But the Statue Maker has something better in mind. He alone knows our Secret Name, and until we learn that name, we're either a mass of frozen potential yet to come alive, or we come alive prematurely, acting out our Given Names because they're the only names we know.

Jacob fell victim to this unhealthy tendency. He wasted far too much headspace thinking, calculating, and scheming about how to obtain a new name. It's why he swindled his brother's birthright out from under him and why he stole his brother's blessing and had to flee his home and everything familiar.

Like so many of us, Jacob wanted to create a new name for himself rather than receive his Secret Name from the Statue Maker. But sadly, through his intense efforts to shirk his Birth Name, he actually came to embody its very meaning: one who supplants and deceives.

All the while, God waited patiently for Jacob.

Eventually, Jacob turned down the noise and listened long enough and hard enough to hear his Secret Name.

Our lives aren't that much different. An entire world is waiting for us to become who we were born to be. The world yearns for us to embrace our destiny. Because when we're alive, everything we touch comes alive too.[1]

Have you ever spent time with someone truly alive?

Such people have a restorative quality about them. Rather than taking energy from others, they're so full of life that they give energy to others.[2] Anchored and centered, people who know their Secret Name are dialed into a different channel and marked by a quiet confidence that allows them to heal the world.

But what sets them apart?

And who gave them permission to dance while the rest of us remain frozen in time?

How do they know what part to play?

In reality, we're the ones playing—they're actually *living*. They know something the rest of us don't.

They know who they are.

They've learned their Secret Name.

And as we'll soon find out, we can too.

3
THE NAME GAME

"What do you do?"

We tend to get asked this question more than any other.

Not "Who do you love?"

Or "What makes you tick?"

Or "What are your dreams?"

Instead, we get a worn-out question that, if we focus on it, puts even more distance between our Secret Name and us.

For many of us, the most important features of a person are external—not about who they are but rather what they have or how they look.

Who has the best job? The nicest car parked at the biggest house? Whose kids dress to impress and make the honor roll? Who still excels at sports, throwing parties, or tithing? Who is the sexiest or savviest?

Although there are exceptions, most men define who they are by what they do—their jobs. Most women define who they are by who they know—their relationships.

Suckered into the Name Game, we focus on externals. We judge and compare and evaluate a person's worth based on the surface level of other people's Given Names.

Who can blame us?

THE NAME GAME

We're human, after all, and it's way easier to look at the size of a guy's bank account or a woman's bra than brave the deep, stormy waters of Secret Names.

That's far too risky and requires some serious emotional excavating. Besides, few of us have done the deep digging in our own lives, and thus we're a bit disqualified from doing it in the lives of others.

As a kid, I was constantly searching for a new name. Every day, the names people gave me pressed down on me like a heavy weight. I hung out with some fairly talented friends, the type of guys whose outer confidence fueled my inner conflict.

Kevin was good at everything: singing, band, sports, and academics. A prodigy, he graduated high school much younger than the rest of us. Then there was Chad. All the girls commented on his looks, sense of humor, and sensitivity. The very fragrance of cool hung on Joel like expensive cologne. When he walked into a room, the suave factor went up at least ten degrees. I could go on and on—Nate, John, Jason—everyone seemed to have an identity they could proudly claim.

Everyone but me.

I was the guy with the girl's name, the skinny guy.

I experimented with a variety of other things, hoping that somehow, somewhere along the way, I'd stumble upon my Secret Name.

In one of my first school memories, I tried my luck as an artist. The teacher charged my entire class with the task of making a bunny rabbit. She gave us brightly colored pipe cleaners, paste, cotton balls, crayons, a paper plate, and some construction paper.

Clueless about the finer points of art, I went for speed.

I cut, pasted, and colored as quickly as my little fingers would let me—and then promptly presented myself and my masterpiece at the teacher's desk, anxiously awaiting her accolades.

"Class," she instructed, "turn your attention up here. Now, Kary finished his project first, and I want you to look very closely at his work."

I stood there, a fragile mess of potential. This was my moment to come alive, my awakening. This would shut all those kids up, especially the ones who made fun of my girl's name.

"Class," she continued, "I must say, in all my years of teaching, this is the absolute . . . worst bunny I've ever seen. Please don't rush your project like Kary did."

I thought about melting into the floor or dying on the spot. Instead, I bit my lip. I distracted myself with pain, rather than settling for tears. I knew crying in front of my classmates would label me for life.

Maybe you know the feeling? Perhaps you bore a similar moment in your own childhood—a time when you withstood uninvited stares of criticism or cynicism?

That day I learned to hold back, to stay in my shell a little longer—better to let *other* people take risks and look foolish.

Still, my desire to learn my Secret Name superseded my desire to play it safe. A few years later I tried out for the Sunshine Kids, a singing group associated with my school. Each kid in the group dressed up in some kind of ethnic clothing and sang, "It's a Small World (After All)" at venues all over the country. The director must have felt sorry for me. She let me into the group even though I couldn't hold a tune.

She picked me to be the German kid. My last name (Oberbrunner) sealed that deal before I could even form an opinion on the matter. I was rewarded with a combination of brownish shorts, tube socks, a white shirt with suspenders, and a silly hat with a red feather in it.

Needless to say, I dropped out of the Sunshine Kids after one performance, and no one seemed sorry to see me go.

THE NAME GAME

In high school, I tried out for the school play—making my debut in my junior year. The cast grew close to each other, almost like a family. But in my senior year, my childhood stuttering demons returned. I left the stage in tears and told the director the next day that I was done. My life had enough drama already. I didn't need to create any more.

Eventually something stuck—or so I thought. I was decent at wrestling, and it seemed like I might have found my niche and perhaps my new name. Despite my childhood asthma, my cardiovascular health surpassed most. I trained unofficially year round, even joining the soccer team just to stay in shape for wrestling.

Although I made some strides my junior year, taking first in some tournaments and making it to state, my career ended early. A freak accident at the conclusion of my senior year—I was jumped in the alley behind my house and received a major concussion just days before the state tournament—caused my parents to bench me, all according to doctor's orders.

As a result, that next year I didn't attend a prestigious college or join the military like my friends. I went to an unaccredited Bible Institute that trained people to serve overseas as missionaries. Nine times out of ten, just applying guaranteed acceptance. Seventy-five bucks a week covered room, board, and tuition. Not that the Bible Institute was a bad choice. I learned critical lessons about life and God. Plus I met many great people. But I didn't find a new name there, and believe me, I tried.

Overcoming the Name Game seemed so easy for the friends I met. They came as freshmen, learned about God, met their true love, got married by their senior semester, and went further in missionary training. Not me.

I tried to make the missionary gig work. But while sitting at a bonfire halfway around the world on a short-term mission trip, I knew that to stay permanently just to play the Name Game would be wrong. I decided then and there that the full-time missionary thing wasn't for me.

YOUR SECRET NAME

After completing my two years at that Bible Institute, I looked into attending college. My choices were a tad restricted due to the fact that only two colleges accepted my non-accredited coursework. Logically, I attended one of them, in small-town Indiana. Things began to click. I aced Greek and Hebrew and knocked a year off seminary. Then, while working on my master's in divinity, I decided to enter the military as a chaplain.

The armed forces always appealed to me. When I was young, a high school senior unofficially mentored me long before it was a buzzword. Although this popular football player eventually graduated, he came back to church on Christmas breaks wearing his uniform from West Point. Even as a young kid, I could tell the military brought with it a certain type of name recognition, and I craved it.

I connected with a certain flavor of church, which agreed to pay for my seminary in exchange for becoming a military chaplain under their banner. I got licensed as a pastor, received my required denominational endorsement, and applied to the Air Force. I could almost hear my new name—LIEUTENANT—and I fancied the way it rolled off the tongue.

I passed my physical with flying colors, but the day I went to sign my papers at the Air Force recruiter's office, my future crumbled before I had enough sense to recognize what just happened. The recruiter led me through a standard questionnaire.

We each had a copy in front of us. She'd read the question from her form, and then I'd check the appropriate box on my form: *Yes* or *No*.

"Have you ever had cancer?" she asked.

"Nope," I replied.

"What about HIV?"

"Nope."

"Asthma?"

"Yep," I answered. "But only as a child. I grew out of it a few years back."

THE NAME GAME

I must have given a wrong answer because the recruiter looked up from her clipboard, promptly stood up, walked out from behind her desk, and abruptly closed the door. After sitting back down, she placed the clipboard on her desk and folded her hands. The mood morphed from tranquil to troubled.

"Let me tell you something," she said, speaking in a solemn tone. "Listen very closely. If you want to get into the Air Force, I suggest you change your answer."

"Why?"

"Since Desert Storm, we've beefed up our standards. Too many soldiers with childhood asthma had adverse reactions to the desert conditions. We don't take chances anymore."

I looked down at my copy of the form. At the top, in black and white, the official papers warned: "Any falsification of information on this document could result in a fine of $10,000 or 5 years in prison."

She leaned in and picked up the pen that I must have dropped. "Here . . . just check 'No.'"

Obediently, I picked up the pen and let it hover over the box.

"Don't worry, Kary. We do this all the time." She shrugged and leaned back with a casual air. "Besides, no one would qualify if they didn't fudge a little." Her laugh seemed forced, almost nervous.

I left childhood and entered adulthood in one single moment. My present circumstances converged with images of my future on the battlefield. But more than that, I remember the internal battle between my emotions and my conscience.

I wanted to find a new name so badly I actually considered following her orders. But the more I thought about the white lie, the more it made me sick. I knew I couldn't base my new career on deception.

Besides, what's in a name if you have to lie in order to receive it?

"I need the weekend to think about it," I stated rigidly. But I knew I wasn't going to budge.

"Fine," she said, standing up. "Take your time. But I'm telling you, they're not going to let you in if you admit to asthma."

I walked out of her office and into the parking lot. I slammed my car door and cursed God. What gave him the right to dangle yet another dream in front of me, only to yank it right back when just inches from my grasp?

Hot tears stung my cheeks. I was so close to learning my new name, finally, and now one check mark stood in my way. I had been convinced becoming a chaplain was the path for paying my seminary tuition. I had signed all the papers with my denomination, and they had already released the funds and introduced me at several functions as the chaplain cadet.

Still, I knew what I had to do. I called the recruiter on Monday and told her I wouldn't lie.

She was right. The Air Force didn't let me in.

Resolved not to quit, I applied for the Army and Navy as well, but they didn't budge either. My application moved up the ladder, all the way to the Pentagon, not because of me but because of my endorsing agent's special connections. Still, the answer was firm. In red letters across my file, it loudly proclaimed—REJECTED.

I'd struck out again. My Secret Name eluded me, slipping right through my fingers. I was left without a new identity—just my Birth Name, and a girl's one at that.

———

Jacob had trouble finding his Secret Name too. Growing up alongside a sibling with natural-born talent didn't ease the ache. Esau, the firstborn, had everything going for him, including being Dad's favorite, an excellent hunter, and exceptionally hairy—all key qualities in primitive cultures. The Scriptures define Esau as a "man of the open country" and a "man of the field." He liked the outdoors, stunk like the outdoors, and he was *covered* in red hair.

Jacob, on the other hand, had smooth, soft skin. In a pastoral culture that valued hard physical labor, such skin was a sign of weakness. Jacob may not have been well liked by his brother, but his mom, Rebekah, preferred him over his older brother, Esau. There's nothing wrong with being a mama's boy, but in antiquity, there were stigmas associated with a man who refrained from hunting and preferred the kitchen instead.

Jacob did both.

He knew more than his fair share about cooking. After all, Esau sold his birthright for a pot of stew cooked by his kid brother. While Esau followed Dad on hunting expeditions, increasing his follicle count and predatory tactics, Jacob hung out in the tent with Mom, using lotion for his smooth hands.

Besides being described as a schemer and supplanter, Jacob is also described as plain and quiet. Quiet can be a good thing, but this wasn't confident-quiet or relaxed-quiet. No, this was fear-quiet. Unknown-quiet. Jacob didn't stand proudly in his quietness. Instead, he hid shamefully behind it.

Strangely, people like Esau often find themselves in more trouble than people like Jacob. When it becomes our defining trait, success can hijack us, whether in terms of looks, talent, athleticism, or money. Sometimes it's the only thing people see.

Maybe *you're* one of these successful people. Maybe your brother or sister is the simple, plain, ordinary one. Maybe you're the one with the looks, the talent, or the brains—the one graced with the killer sense of humor or the artistic eye. Your angst is just as profound and your pain is just as pronounced as Jacob's.

Each of us—no matter our Given Names—must learn our Secret Name. Because beneath the *surface* of every person is a human being with an insatiable need to know who he or she was created to be.

Just listen to Esau's heartache—the successful brother—when his father, Isaac, tells him he can't grant his son his Secret Name. "When Esau heard his father's words, he burst out with a loud and bitter cry and said to his father, 'Bless me—me too, my father!' "

Your grief may be just as deep, your reply just as bitter. But our earthly father isn't the one who grants us our Secret Name. This type of name must fall from the lips of Another.

PART TWO

Accepting the Present

*And I'm sure there's something in a shade of gray
Something in between,
And I can always change my name, if that's what you mean.*

—"Anna Begins," Counting Crows

4
PUPPETS AND PAWNS

Forty miles from my wife's hometown, a tragic story recently broke about a father who committed horrible acts against his son.

Maybe you think you can guess what happened? Perhaps he taught his son how to steal or made him work the street corner selling drugs or, worse yet, his body. Regrettably, these are crimes we've heard about before and their shock value has faded—not intentionally, but simply because they play out in real time in every country, in every city, every day.

This father, however, did something different, something we'd never heard before: he injected his thirteen-year-old son with steroids. This father, who shared custody of his son due to a divorce, started him "on a regimen of vitamins, human growth hormone, and steroids in hopes that he would excel at skating."[1]

This father eventually secured his dream the moment his son secured his victory.

But at what cost?

The son inherited a fractured relationship with his father, not to mention a two-year expulsion from the sport. His dad received a six-year prison sentence from a federal judge, and upon release, he'll remain on probation for another four years—required to complete up to 500 hours of community service.[2]

All this pain—physical, relational, emotional—for one single Given Name: NATIONAL CHAMPION.

Who's to blame?

Most of us run to ridicule the father as both heartless and hurtful. Of course, we should hold such parents accountable. They're guilty of using their kids as puppets and pawns to advance their own agenda.

But what if we look a little deeper and think a little longer?

Maybe these parents are caught up in the Name Game too?

Maybe they're hoping to carve out a new name just like the rest of us.

Maybe they want to distinguish themselves and their longing is so acute that they're willing to hurt themselves and their children.

Suddenly the dad who shot his kid with steroids makes perfect sense.

Perhaps skating started out as a type of bonding activity for father and son. The tournaments on the road, the new hotels, the cross-country flights, and the competitions brought father and son together. But soon none of that could quiet the ache any longer. Trophies took over, and first place became the focus. The only thing that mattered was winning because that was the only way to score a new identity—FATHER OF A NATIONAL CHAMPION.

But such names never satisfy.

Recently, a mom asked a bunch of us on Facebook to vote for her daughter. Her twenty-something daughter was a finalist in a potential Superbowl commercial. In the short thirty-second clip, you can guess how she was portrayed—not for her brains. I don't think the mom realized that she was positioning her daughter as an *object* for us to evaluate, rather than an eternal soul to understand.

Many years ago, I became a pawn in someone else's Name Game. Senior night at my Bible Institute—guys in ties, girls in dresses—we sat with our teachers at tables with linen napkins and candles. Spread before us, the banquet and the world were ready for our consumption.

After dinner, the emcee explained a tradition. "Your teachers would love to hear about your plans after graduation," he said. "Simply stand up at your table one at a time, and state your name and future plans."

Pretty simple, I thought.

But when I remembered one of my teachers was seated next to me, my tie suddenly felt a tad restricting against my Adam's apple. Deciphering my "future plans" wasn't a simple task. I didn't have a clue about what I was doing for breakfast, much less the following year.

The only thing I had definitely ruled *out* was missionary work overseas—not the type of activity you should rule out as a student at *this* Bible Institute since it was pumped into our heads 24/7. I got the feeling that if I didn't go out of the country, there was something wrong with me—like I was disobedient and running from God just like Jonah and the story about the big fish.

And I knew what happened to Jonah.

Not every teacher made me feel this way. Many were balanced and motivated by grace. These teachers had already discovered their Secret Names. Unfortunately, the teacher sitting next to me that night was not one of those. He was cut from another cloth.

One day in class, he told all of us that his wife's health prevented him from serving as a missionary overseas. When he told us this, he crumpled up in tears as if he had just committed a horrible sin. He broke the news to us with the severity of a political sex scandal, his face depleted and embarrassed. "You students *must* go in my place," he sobbed, layering the guilt on pretty thick. "You must go!"

"We'll start up here at the table in the front, to my left," the emcee said. Our tranquil banquet transformed into a big ball of anxiety. As the first senior stood to share, I noticed my teacher fumbling in his sport coat, obviously searching for something. After a moment or two, he pulled out a pen and a small pad of paper. My eyes locked onto his distracting movements as he proceeded to draw a line straight down the middle of his paper.

The first senior to brave the spotlight, unaware of the little conspiracy unfolding in the back of the room, stood. "My plans are to go on to language school and then head to the mission field." The room responded with nods of affirmation.

Scribble.

My teacher made a small vertical mark on the left side of the column.

The next student stood up promptly. "I plan on going back home and help my dad with his business."

Scribble.

This time he checked the right side of the column.

After a dozen or so seniors shared their future plans, I finally caught on to what my teacher was doing. If a senior shared about heading toward the mission field, they made it to the left side of the column. But, if a senior shared about doing anything else—attending college, starting a family, or working a "secular" job—they made it to the right side of the column.

My mind reeled. I had a hard time comprehending the Name Game unraveling right before me. How could this teacher categorize us?

My turn snuck up on me, ready or not. My legs felt like cement blocks, but I managed to coax them into cooperating, and they eventually obeyed my command to stand. The pace of my speech was observably slow. "Hi . . . everyone . . . uhh . . . hmmm . . . my future plans are . . ."

Looking down, I saw my teacher sitting next to me with his pen poised, ready to label me. Although disappointed and distracted, I wasn't willing to buckle.

```
|||| |||| ||||  |  |||| |||| ||||
||||             |  |||| ///
```

I started again. "My future plans are . . ." I got tripped up again, but only momentarily.

"My plans are . . . to make it through the end of the day."

Not a sound. Not a shuffle. Not even a sigh.

Then chuckles broke out, and soon a rousing applause—the entire room clapped enthusiastically.

Did they think I was trying to be funny?

Or perhaps they appreciated my simplicity?

Were they, like me, sick of feeling the pressure to perform?

I looked down at my teacher, now momentarily frozen, his jaw hanging open much farther than he would have been comfortable with had he seen himself in a mirror. He didn't know how to respond. Then, rather abruptly, he put his pen down in disgust and looked away.

I didn't intend to embarrass him. I just knew I had to be honest about my lack of clarity regarding my future plans. I wasn't about to make something up just to please my teacher. I knew he wanted me to be his puppet and pawn, but instead of spite, I felt sorrow.

He wasn't the villain, but rather a victim.

Like me and like the dad who injected his son with steroids, he too was trying to win at the Name Game. What he failed to realize was that no amount of marks on the left side of his notebook could give him the identity he craved. He needed to hear the Father's gentle whisper, just like the rest of us.

Head back to the beginning of the Bible and the storyline sounds like a bad rerun. The patriarch Isaac loved Esau not for who he was but for what he did—specifically hunting. Notice the text, "Isaac loved Esau, because he had a taste for game."

How degrading—to be loved solely because of your ability to retrieve food. Even pets are loved for more compelling reasons, like companionship and comfort.

Not Esau.

He wasn't even loved for his talent, but exclusively to satisfy his father's appetite. As long as the food kept coming, the love kept flowing. The door to dad's heart was solely through his stomach.

Isaac "loved" older son Esau, while his wife, Rebekah, "loved" younger son Jacob.

But was her love conditional too? Was it based on the fact that he hung around the house? Was Jacob a surrogate spouse, privy to private times when Mom downloaded her deepest thoughts and fears?

Although the Scriptures are silent on this point, they're quite outspoken on another one. Years earlier, before either son's birth, Rebekah received a strange prophecy. The Lord said to her, "Two nations are in your womb, and two peoples from within you will be separated; one people will be stronger than the other, and the older will serve the younger."

Perhaps Rebekah clung to Jacob because she knew that Jacob would end up on top. Perhaps she despised Isaac's preferential treatment of Esau and felt Jacob needed an advocate. Maybe Isaac never took his wife's prophecy seriously, and she resented him for it. In any case, we'll consider later how Jacob became Rebekah's pawn in order to ensure the prophecy. Evidently, she convinced herself that God needed her help.

A closer peek proves that Rebekah hardly had Jacob's best interests in mind. In this particular family, people were objects, merely tools to position and arrange like pieces on a chessboard in hopes of securing a win. Lying, scheming, and leveraging defined their interactions.

Perhaps you can relate?

Maybe in your family, the children were bargaining chips during a divorce. Or maybe your parents stayed together, but substituted intimacy with each other for intimacy with you and your siblings. Maybe the climate in your household seemed a little off, the temperature a tad too hot or too cold. Not until adulthood were you able to piece all the clues together—and recognize that you were being used.

Your dad or mom might not have even realized what they were doing at the time—few do. Parents rarely set out to use their sons and daughters. And each parent is the product of imperfect parents too. Most never learned their Secret Names either— and most don't know they don't know.

The vast majority of us are content with our ignorance, unwilling to pursue our Secret Names. Often we think nothing of this price because we're more in tune with our stomach pains than our soul ache. We think more often of our need for food than our need for freedom.

That's what Esau did.

He let his stomach get the best of him, listening more to his urges than to his better judgment. He sold his birthright for a bowl of stew. On the verge of tasting a new name, Esau preferred a meal instead.

Of course, he felt sorry after the exchange. Deception, especially deception by a family member, always leaves a bitter aftertaste.

Jacob, the culinary type, hung around home cooking stew. Esau came in from the open country, famished. Rather than greeting his bro, he got right down to business. His hunger pains outdid any attempt at flattery. The only buttering up on his brain was not directed at a person but a piece of bread accompanying his brother's meal. "Quick," he said to Jacob, "let me have some of that red stew! I'm famished!"

Jacob saw a slight window, always aware of the soul ache that plagued him.

Seizing the opportunity, Jacob replied, "First sell me your birthright."

The meal deal was set: Esau craved stew and Jacob craved a new name. But Esau had a few brain cells in addition to his brawn, and he tried to bluff by downplaying the deal. "Look, I am about to die. What good is the birthright to me?"

Ever the scheming salesman, Jacob held his ground. "Swear to me first."

In that culture, verbal oaths held legal weight. Esau eventually took the bait and the bowl. He swore an oath, selling his birthright to Jacob. Esau wolfed down his meal and then left his brother's kitchen—both parties happy with the transaction.

But that wasn't the end.

The moment his hunger pains subsided, Esau's angst sprang up. He felt deceived, angry, and betrayed. That's what usually happens when we stop stuffing our faces and get in touch with the starved state of our souls.

He was too late.

Jacob clung to that birthright with the same tenacity as a lion clings to a recent kill—the birthright his ticket to a brighter horizon and quite possibly a new name. In antiquity, birthrights meant much more than bragging rights—signifying a double inheritance, for starters. But more than money, a birthright also carried spiritual privileges too, namely the responsibility of family priest, a critical role within the Jewish tradition. Firstborns were also endowed with the "judicial authority of his father."[3]

If you were the firstborn male in the family, you pretty much struck the lottery—the size of your smile contingent only on the size of your father's bank account.[4]

"First begotten" meant first in importance.[5] In your father's eyes, a birthright signified that you were worthy of more materially, spiritually, and judicially, and Jacob—the plain, ordinary, scheming, deceiving young man—desperately wanted to be more in the eyes of his father.

True, Esau was his father's puppet, but he also was the object of Isaac's love. Jacob knew this. That's why stealing Esau's birthright took shape as a covert operation, an attempt to secure his father's love and attention. But even though Jacob swindled his older brother Esau out of his birthright, he failed to realize the lesson I learned at the Air Force recruiter's office. *What's in a name if you have to lie in order to receive it?*

As long as we're content pretending to be someone we're not, we'll never discover our Secret Name. When we need to lie in order to get a new name, we only fool one person.

Ourselves.

And we end up chalking up one more Given Name—IMPOSTER.

5

IMPOSTER SYNDROME

Who am I?
When trying to answer this critical question, most of us tend to look in every direction but the right one.

Sometimes we look inward—via mirrors.

Mirrors *do* serve a purpose. They tell us how we look. Unfortunately, they have their limitations. They can't tell us who we are—despite how intently we peer into them. Mirrors might help us see our misplaced hair or perhaps that our hair is *missing*, but they can't reflect our true identities.

And so we look outward—to people.

Others *do* give their unsolicited impressions regarding who they *think* we are. We often digest their impressions and convince ourselves to be satisfied with the trivial terms they grant us. This fuels our addiction to affirmation, motivates us to work long hours, and convinces us to buy the latest lotion that promises to reverse the effects of aging—because as long as the performance keeps flowing, so do the Given Names.

But the truth is, looking only in one direction—upward—will reveal our Secret Name. Fellow humans, no matter how loud they speak, can never replace the voice of the Father. And mirrors, no matter how sparkling they appear, can never clear up the fog. God's whisper alone satisfies our soul ache because God alone knows us better than we know ourselves.

Looking in any other direction for cues on who we are only accentuates the hypocrisy and duplicity that inhabit our hearts. Hypocrisy—because nobody completely bridges the chasm between what we say and how we act. Duplicity—because on some levels, we're all imposters.

Intentionally or unintentionally, we all wear a certain set of masks. Partial disclosure isn't bad all the time because it protects us from shame and embarrassment. But many of us wear our masks far too frequently—and we've lost touch with our potential for who God created us to be.

In one season of my life, this described my dilemma. I didn't allow my feet to hit the floor in the morning without first strapping on my masks—my survival dependent on my undisclosed ritual. Unbeknownst to me, living as a perpetual imposter brought with it a tremendous price.

Wearing my masks put an enormous space between my Secret Name and me. I needed them though because my masks served their exact purpose. They *masked* the pain that would've pushed me to the Father if I only had let him into my pain. Instead, I pushed him away and, in exchange, became infatuated with inflicting pain on myself.

I descended into a twisted addiction in which I played the part of perpetrator and victim, all wrapped into one. I settled for life as a self-injurer, fixated on cutting my own skin, and I almost destroyed myself in the process.

―――∞―――

Despite the fact that no one foresaw the warning signs, my college life came crashing down around me. I felt like a stranger in my own skin—my problem accentuated by taking cues from others. People seemed to have me pegged, walking around with a better handle on *me* than I did.

Although others spouted only inaccurate impressions, this tendency still proved unnerving. I realized people prefer to define us by what we do rather than take the time to discover who we are. Titles serve a quicker fix, which allows others to classify us without actually understanding us.

Honestly, though, even if I had known who I was in that time and space, I doubt I would have felt comfortable walking around without my masks.

Authenticity is hard enough as it is, but small communities can often exacerbate the problem. Couple that with places that stereotypically punish prodigals and reward plastic performances, and you have a real predicament on your hands.

Within such institutions reside a few pilgrims bold enough to voice their questions and express their struggles. Yet this remnant rarely stands before the masses or the microphones. Instead, they're dug into foxholes, bruised and bloodied, often wounded by their own army.

Such souls model brave individuality and honesty, but they're also labeled as dangerous folk who shouldn't be emulated. While I admired them from afar, I was far too busy doing "the right thing" to seriously consider them. I only knew a world in need of saving—even if it meant losing my own soul in the process.

And so I mastered the art of pretending.

While I felt entangled by expectations and the Given Names that came my way, the incentives, manifested in the form of leadership positions, kept coming, and there wasn't appropriate space to admit I was UNKNOWN on the inside.

Although I was unsure about a whole bunch of issues, the people around me didn't seem to notice. Relatively quickly, I inherited even more labels—RESIDENT ASSISTANT, JUNIOR CLASS VICE PRESIDENT, and STUDENT CHAPLAIN.

If you're tempted to be impressed, don't be.

I'm not belittling these titles. Believe me, I wanted them—even interviewing for some and out-performing my peers in order to get them. And I'm not disrespecting the leaders who gave me these names. Yet even as I took on new roles, confusion clung to me like smoke in one of those old crowded bowling alleys. No matter how many showers I took, when I was alone, I could still smell the stench.

Within some of these public roles, I spoke to the entire student body on issues related to God and faith. For as much confidence as I exuded on the outside, I felt completely clueless on the inside. In chapel, I might have instructed people about finding their true identity, but back in my dorm room, I felt like a lost little boy. Only semi-content with existing as an imposter, I still didn't feel like playing the part of whistle-blower, calling out my own house of cards.

Besides, the ladders kept coming, and so I kept climbing.

Soon a church allowed me to serve as their pastoral intern, and overnight I inherited the oversight of an entire college ministry—only one year out of college myself. With that position came elder's meetings, board meetings, and pastor's conferences. At the age of twenty-three, I became head pastor of my first church despite the fact that a large percentage of the members were well over seventy years old.

Ready for anything, at my disposal I kept a stockpile of Given Names: CHAPLAIN, LICENSED ELDER, SEMINARIAN, BIBLE STUDENT, PASTOR, COUNSELOR. But in my soul, I knew none of these was my Secret Name.

Who was I fooling?

Everyone—except myself.

I tasted this discrepancy on a daily basis, even before a well-balanced breakfast. And even though I didn't set out to deceive anyone, the higher I climbed, the more I needed to insulate and isolate myself from the truth—mainly, that I was a tourist, only sporadically vacationing in my own life.

Because looking outward toward other people's impressions didn't offer any solace, I turned my attention inward. At first, I found a bit of comfort with introspective contemplation. But not long after, while gazing into a mirror, I merely felt disgust with what I observed—a boy without a name.

As a result, I dialed into a private dialogue with myself. The only parties privy to this discussion were my body and soul, for once both involved in the same conversation. I found comfort in carving my own skin.

Unfortunately, my toxic obsession obtained only one result, one more Given Name—CUTTER.

Um—I take that back.

Although I kept my dark habit under wraps, I inherited one additional result—scars. In those lonely moments, colored with a distinct ritualistic red, I felt real, even if only for an instant. The rest of the time, I preferred IMPOSTER.

I wore *that* name well, and no one could tell it wasn't my color. My synthetic show offered appeal, mainly anesthesia from the ache of not knowing my Secret Name.

Make no mistake.

I never shirked my leadership positions. Rather, I took them quite seriously—actually too seriously. My quandary took root in a different direction—that my Given Names were never enough. These titles had potential to direct me, but I asked too much of them. I begged them to define me, satisfied solely with knowing what I did rather than discovering who I was created to be.

As a result, I often felt like a fake.

Our friend Jacob, the schemer, could relate. Except in his case, he didn't just feel like an imposter. He was one—and a convincing one at that.

Following Jacob's and Esau's meal deal, a rift formed in their already rocky relationship. Who knows how Mom and Dad felt about the birthright exchanged for a bowl of stew. Maybe they believed the deal was fair and square, simple bartering between brothers. But I doubt it.

Understanding the financial, spiritual, and judicial implications of birthrights in the era of antiquity, I'm surprised these brothers still managed to live in the same zip code. Did they look at each other while reclining around the table, or did they simply ignore one another while they waited for Dad to die so they could cash in on their inheritance? For the first time in recorded history, Esau, the older brother, would receive one-third, while Jacob, the younger brother, would get two-thirds.

We know Esau felt deeply betrayed by Jacob, his brother, evidenced in his emotional plea: "Isn't he rightly named Jacob? He has deceived me . . . He took my birthright."

Circumstances soon went from bad to worse. Father Isaac wasn't getting any younger. He was blind and unable to do much of anything. Consistent with tradition, Isaac wanted to bless his eldest son before taking his final breath. Even though Jacob had stolen Esau's *birthright*, Isaac still felt compelled to *bless* his favorite son, Esau.

Birthrights carried with them legal ramifications related to the hard numbers of inheriting possessions—like donkeys, camels, and crops. But blessings were something a little different, related to the mystical and the soft science of inheriting prophecies—like the unknown and the yet to be discovered.

Isaac knew Jacob had secured his future flocks. The meal deal made that possible. However, in his mind, the prophetic spirit surrounding the patriarchal blessing still seemed wide open, able to be dispensed to the son of his choosing.[1] And no one—especially Jacob—had to guess which son Isaac would choose to receive the blessing.

Isaac said to Esau, "I am now an old man and don't know the day of my death. Now then, get your weapons—your quiver and bow—and go out to the open country to hunt some wild game for me. Prepare me the kind of tasty food I like and bring it to me to eat, so that I may give you my blessing before I die."

Even on his deathbed, Isaac still viewed Esau for what he did rather than who he was. Like any son, Esau longed for a transformational relationship with his father, but all he received was a transactional one. And so Esau left home in search of some wild game, knowing that upon his successful return, a new name would be waiting on the lips of his earthly father—after Dad downed his dinner, of course.

Ironically, these events never happened. A conspiracy of epic proportions hid right behind the nearest tent flap.

Rebekah kept her ears peeled as she bustled around the family compound. In the past, her good listening skills probably helped her keep the peace around the house. But on this day, her eavesdropping fractured the family for good. She heard the entire dialogue between Isaac and Esau. Not liking what she perceived, she went straight to Jacob.

Rebekah said to her son Jacob, "Look, I overheard your father say to your brother Esau, 'Bring me some game and prepare me some tasty food to eat, so that I may give you my blessing in the presence of the Lord before I die.'"

Mom cooked up a succulent plan, garnished with layers of delicious deceit. "Now, my son, listen carefully and do what I tell you: Go out to the flock and bring me two choice young goats, so I can prepare some tasty food for your father, just the way he likes it. Then take it to your father to eat, so that he may give you his blessing before he dies."

Despite dishonesty on a grand scale, Rebekah didn't think much of it. The Name Game provoked everyone to outwit each other in the interest of attaining their own agenda.

A schemer knows one when he sees one, and Jacob saw a crack in Mom's conspiracy. He warned, "But my brother Esau is a hairy man, and I'm a man with smooth skin. What if my father touches me? I would appear to be tricking him and would bring down a curse on myself rather than a blessing."

Jacob knew the price of pretending to be someone else. In ancient times, a curse carried as much weight as a blessing. Good thing Mom had things covered: Jacob would strap goatskins to his arms and thereby fool his incapacitated father. She said to him, "My son, let the curse fall on me. Just do what I say; go and get them for me."

She vowed to take care of everything: the food, the hairy arms, and even the outdoor-odor that characterized Esau. If the plot blew up, she'd take the blame.

With conscience quelled—at least temporarily—Jacob got busy. "So he went and got them and brought them to his mother, and she prepared some tasty food, just the way his father liked it. Then Rebekah took the best clothes of Esau her older son, which she had in the house, and put them on her younger son Jacob."

"The best clothes of Esau . . . *which she had in her house*"? The sacred text implies that Rebekah hadn't cooked up this plan instantly—not even overnight. Her slick scheme motivated her to stow away a set of Esau's clothes just for such an occasion. She even took the precaution to "vacuum seal" the garments in order to preserve the stench.

"She also covered his hands and the smooth part of his neck with the goatskins. Then she handed to her son Jacob the tasty food and the bread she had made."

With the same normalcy of a mom packing her son a lunch and then sending him off to school, Rebekah sent her son off to swindle his father, which, of course, was *her* husband.

"He went to his father and said, 'My father.'

" 'Yes, my son,' he answered. 'Who is it?'

"Jacob said to his father, 'I am Esau your firstborn. I have done as you told me. Please sit up and eat some of my game so that you may give me your blessing.' "

Jacob played the role of imposter so well that his own father didn't suspect anything—at least at first. "Isaac asked his son, 'How did you find it so quickly, my son?'"

Jacob didn't skip a beat. "'The Lord your God gave me success,' he replied."

Having spent a lifetime scheming, it was second nature to Jacob, just as it is to some of us. But notice what Jacob revealed with his word choice. Not "the Lord *my* God" or even simply "the Lord God." Instead, Jacob used the pronoun *your*. He had yet to experience God for himself. The whole "God thing" was Mom's and Dad's gig—not his.

Perhaps sensing something was not quite right, Jacob's father called him closer. "Isaac said to Jacob, 'Come near so I can touch you, my son, to know whether you really are my son Esau or not.' Jacob went close to his father Isaac, who touched him and said, 'The voice is the voice of Jacob, but the hands are the hands of Esau.'"

Holding his breath, Jacob realized Mom's plan was working. "Are you really my son Esau?" Isaac asked.

"I am," Jacob replied.

Isaac's heart told him the truth: this wasn't Esau. But his stomach, as always, carried the day. "Then he said, 'My son, bring me some of your game to eat, so that I may give you my blessing.' Jacob brought it to him and he ate; and he brought some wine and he drank. Then his father Isaac said to him, 'Come here, my son, and kiss me.' So he went to him and kissed him. When Isaac caught the smell of his clothes, he blessed him."

"[Isaac] said, 'Ah, the smell of my son is like the smell of a field that the Lord has blessed. May God give you of heaven's dew and of earth's richness—an abundance of grain and new wine. May nations serve you and peoples bow down to you. Be lord over your brothers, and may the sons of your mother bow down to you. May those who curse you be cursed and those who bless you be blessed.'"

And with that, it was all over. Jacob had won again, previously securing his brother's birthright and now his blessing. Little did Jacob know that Secret Names can't be stolen.

"After Isaac finished blessing him and Jacob had scarcely left his father's presence, his brother Esau came in from hunting. He too prepared some tasty food and brought it to his father. Then he said to him, 'My father, sit up and eat some of my game, so that you may give me your blessing.'"

Esau held up his end of the bargain. In his mind, his moment of grandeur was about to make a grand entrance. He was on the cusp of receiving his reward and his new name. Little did Esau know that Secret Names can't be purchased.

"His father Isaac asked him, 'Who are you?' 'I am your son,' he answered, 'your firstborn, Esau.' Isaac trembled violently and said, 'Who was it, then, that hunted game and brought it to me? I ate it just before you came and I blessed him — and indeed he will be blessed!'"

Isaac "trembled *violently*"!

Blessings are that big—big enough to alter future generations.

Isaac knew it. Esau knew it. And Jacob knew it too.

"When Esau heard his father's words, he burst out with a loud and bitter cry and said to his father, 'Bless me—me too, my father!' But [Isaac] said, 'Your brother came deceitfully and took your blessing.' Esau said, 'Isn't he rightly named Jacob? He has deceived me these two times: He took my birthright, and now he's taken my blessing!' Then he asked, 'Haven't you reserved any blessing for me?' Isaac answered Esau, 'I have made him lord over you and have made all his relatives his servants, and I have sustained him with grain and new wine. So what can I possibly do for you, my son?'"

Although desperately wanting to help his older son, Isaac knew he couldn't reverse the blessing. With Jacob's future secured and the blessing already bestowed, only one name remained for Esau—UNKNOWN.

6

TILL WE HAVE NAMES

My friend Allie took a trip to Kenya in 2005. She partnered with the Joni and Friends Ministry to provide Bibles and wheelchairs for those with special needs in Kenya. Her team's greatest prayer request was that each needy person could be given a wheelchair that fit properly, as an improper fit causes bedsores.

For most of us, wheelchairs hardly seem like a luxury. Yet in many parts of the world, a wheelchair means entrance into independence—no longer having to rely on friends and family to carry you through life. In Kenya, people with disabilities suffer intense shame and neglect. Sadly, children with special needs are often hidden in households or even abandoned, as parents are unable to cope with the financial and emotional burdens.

While on the trip, Allie met a boy in his late teens who lay naked on his urine-soaked hospital bed. Raw bedsores covered his body. His knees remained locked toward his body, forcing him into a fetal position. He arrived at the hospital in 2001, without a past and without a name.

The hospital workers had hoped to do him a favor by not naming him. Their logic? If anyone came looking for him, an incorrect name would complicate the proceedings. As a result, they simply referred to him as "UNKNOWN."

His story and his face were seared into Allie's psyche. She quickly learned life in Kenya was bad enough without the use of your legs, but not having a name bordered on inhumane. To be UNKNOWN was to be unloved, uncared for, and unnamed. UNKNOWN signified utter isolation.

Rabbi Daniel Lapin, a noted Jewish scholar, believes namelessness is as dehumanizing as slavery. He explains, "This opening of the Book of Exodus . . . with its curious absence of names, demonstrates this important equation: Slavery = no names. It is just as true to say that when you deprive people of names, you are creating circumstances of slavery."[1]

Perhaps this is why many prisons and concentration camps strip people of their names. In place of names, prisoners are assigned numbers. This intentional strategy for dehumanizing demoralizes and discourages individuals. When people lose their *names*, they often lose their independence, individuality, and identity as well.

The outward pain of "UNKNOWN," the Kenyan boy, paralleled with the inward pain of Jacob and Esau. "UNKNOWN" lay crippled, his entire body covered with sores, while the twins lay emotionally crippled, their souls covered with sores. Both Jacob and Esau had several Given Names, but neither of these men knew their Secret Name.

In a real sense, they also wore the name UNKNOWN.

In the last chapter, we left Jacob and Esau—and their entire family—plunging off a relational cliff.

Jacob played the loser's part. Even though he secured his father's blessing, he had lied in order to get it. How could he respect himself, performing as Mom's pawn one more time—exchanging betrayal for blessing? Jacob thought he'd secured a bright future, but he'd created a horrible past in order to achieve it.

Then there was Esau.

He played the puppet *again* and came up short *again*—his Secret Name eluding him one more time. I wonder how Esau slept after that ultimate deception? This wasn't the first time his brother had swindled him, but he swore it would be the last. The Old Testament informs us that "Esau held a grudge against Jacob because of the blessing his father had given him. He said to himself, 'The days of mourning for my father are near; then I will kill my brother Jacob.'"

Esau generously decided to wait until Dad died before taking his brother out. But he was unable to keep his intentions secret. The Scriptures say, "When Rebekah was told what her older son Esau had said, she sent for her younger son Jacob and said to him, 'Your brother Esau is consoling himself with the thought of killing you.'"

Consoling himself?

The writer uses the Hebrew word *nacham*, often translated "comfort," in order to explain how Esau was making it through life—by comforting himself with the thought of killing Jacob. Walking around without a name can be *that* toxic.

Living as an "UNKNOWN" often leads to some behavior that Jesus warned about. "The thief comes only to steal and kill and destroy"—and the thief in this passage is none other than Satan.

When he was created, Satan already had a name, and a good one at that: Lucifer, meaning "morning star." But Satan wanted a new name, and so he attempted to forge one on his own.

> *You said in your heart, "I will ascend to heaven; I will raise my throne above the stars of God; I will sit enthroned on the mount of assembly, on the utmost heights of the sacred mountain. I will ascend above the tops of the clouds; I will make myself like the Most High."*
>
> Isaiah 14:13–14

You probably know how his corrupted coup went down. No longer fit for heaven, God cast Lucifer down to earth. "The great dragon was hurled down—that ancient serpent called the devil, or Satan, who leads the whole world astray. He was hurled to the earth, and his angels with him."

Unsuccessful in securing his own Secret Name, Satan has been scheming ever since. Using people as his puppets and pawns, Satan has infiltrated earth, wooing us away from finding our Secret Name in the only legitimate place—within a relationship with the heavenly Father.

Instead, he tempts us to carve our own path and manufacture a Secret Name by our own strength. This strategy, originally exported in Eden, lured Adam and Eve away from God and promised that they instead could become their own gods.

> *Now the serpent was more crafty than any of the wild animals the Lord God had made. He said to the woman, "Did God really say, 'You must not eat from any tree in the garden'?" The woman said to the serpent, "We may eat fruit from the trees in the garden, but God did say, 'You must not eat fruit from the tree that is in the middle of the garden, and you must not touch it, or you will die.' " "You will not surely die," the serpent said to the woman. "For God knows that when you eat of it your eyes will be opened, and you will be like God, knowing good and evil."*
>
> Genesis 3:1–5

Adam and Eve fell for the original meal deal, centuries before Esau did. In an effort to buy their Secret Names, humanly speaking they gave up their chance of actually obtaining them. They carved their own path, but unfortunately one without much potential.

Throughout history, humanity has imitated Adam and

Eve's bad example. Such was the case for Jacob's life and, regrettably, for mine as well.

When I was twenty-one, I used to drive to my favorite place to think about being a boy without a name: a graveyard in the middle of nowhere. I drove deserted roads. I listened to brooding music. I cut myself. I wrote in my journal—all in a desperate effort to dislodge emotions buried deep inside. As a kid brimming with anger and unease, I had yet to become fluent in the language of feelings.

Cutting wasn't some sadistic fad I stumbled into. No one knew about my covert addiction. Rather, self-mutilation was a complex dialogue I had exclusively with myself. Multifaceted on many levels, cutting offered me a couple of things: like a "release," for starters.

Convinced that bringing rage or frustration to God was irreverent, I stuffed down my displeasure with him and his world. Still, every once in a while, the stuffing had to stop—not because I wanted it to stop, just that I couldn't put the pain any other place. Overwhelmed and overpowered, the pain had to go somewhere. For me, it flowed out through the blade of a knife.

I felt empty and destitute inside, my fabricated facial expressions deceiving everyone. As an imposter, I was a prisoner in my own skin, unable to identify the bars that boxed me in. I cringed every time I heard my Given Names—PASTOR, COUNSELOR, SEMINARIAN. These terms hardly depicted me and only extended the lie. I quickly despised the new titles as soon as I got them because these names were never enough.

Journaling offered some solace. Still, at times pen and paper fell far short. In these moments of emotional overload, I felt like a fraud attempting to use words, knowing full well they simply weren't enough. My pain too deep, my words too shallow, and my anger too great, I needed to see red blood rather than blue or black ink.

Cutting allowed my insides to come out, surfacing forbidden unknown areas. Self-injury enabled me to achieve authenticity, even if only for an instant. My arms and legs a type of canvas, my blade awakened the artist within.

Some cutters make horizontal or vertical lines across their skin, nothing more and nothing less, but I craved something greater. Although I made lines, more often I carved words into my body—names, you might say. I felt so clueless and messed up that seeing some identity imprinted on my arm in crimson script somehow eased the ache.

My journal captured a portion of my angst:

ALL IS

All I am is here.
All I want is you.
All I contain are essences and fabrics of my objects of
    hatred that are rooted so deep.

All I desire is death.
All I demand is cure.
All I see is pain and anger, the consummation of two
    bodies, two worlds. They only offer confusion.

All I hate is me.
All I kill is you.
All I perceive is torture and diseases of illness that distorts
    and disrupts how I see you.

All I feel is emptiness.
All I cut is sin.
All I give is my actions of heartless devotion and cold
    compassion. This world is ice.

All I crush is life.
All I bleed is trash.
All I know I cannot get from my head to my heart and thus I am cursed, a permanent visitor in my prison.

All I consume is tears.
All I cry is contempt.
All I say are slices upon my arms. Self-mutilation is the only way to express the hate I have.

All I possess is question.
All I persist is uncertainty.
All I pretend is now surfacing. And all that remains is the blood fresh upon the floor.

All I know is life.
All I reach is air.
All I embrace is emptiness, condemnation, and rejection. And the most comforting friend is pain.

In my safe graveyard, names carved on stone-cold marble and granite stood out proudly and permanently, a stark contrast from temporary titles that littered my life. I tried to carve more lasting names on my stone-cold body—but even those scars faded, and I'd drive to my graveyard yet again.

Blaise Pascal wrote, "All the unhappiness of men arises from one single fact, that they cannot stay quietly in their own [room]."[2] Despite agreeing with that assessment, I made sure I never stayed in my room alone. Instead, I stayed way too busy at school and work, oblivious to the fact that I was speeding toward a wall without any brakes.

The crash came later that spring—a crash I now understand was layered in love. At the time, I couldn't hear the Father's gentle whisper, so he decided to change his tone.

I had just finished an intense academic stretch, completing coursework and tackling a slew of exams. As I looked toward moving from an interim pastor to full-time while entering my final year of seminary and getting married two months after that, my stress levels soared to an all-time high. During a semester break, I decided to visit my parents in their new house.

I knew Mom and Dad were headed out for the evening, so when I arrived I fumbled around in the detached garage looking for the promised hide-a-key. Tracing the ledge above my head, my fingers felt in the darkness for the thin ridges. Just as I found it, I clumsily knocked it to the floor. Kneeling in the pitch-black, I eventually found the key, even as my anxiety ramped higher and higher.

After a frustratingly long time, I ventured to the back door and found the lock. Quickly, I inserted the key and pushed open the door—only to find myself in the same uninviting darkness, but now in an unfamiliar kitchen. With a duffel bag over my shoulder and a dirty laundry bag weighing down my white-knuckled fist, I struggled to find a light switch.

The more I looked, the more afraid I became—not simply of the darkness, but of my entire way of life. Throughout my childhood, "home" was a concept that evoked security and comfort. All that had converged with this present moment. I already felt out of control, and now I was a stranger in a strange house. My parents' new place was a physical representation of how little I knew myself, and the interior darkness was simply unbearable.

That's when I lost it.

A huge wave of fear submerged me. Having reached my limit, I felt completely overwhelmed.

My breathing quickened.

My heart raced.

My face burned up.

The room around me and the thoughts inside me spun wild. Minutes before only a boy without a name, now I was also a boy without a home, adrift on an ocean of apprehension and ignorance. I confronted a disconcerting thought head-on. I was all alone in this world.

Slumped against the wall, caught in a panic attack, I called my father on the phone.

Grasping for words, all I could find were tears. Sensing something was deeply wrong, my parents left their banquet and raced home. I lay unmoving in the darkness for minutes that seemed like hours.

Upon their return, my parents provided as much support as they could. They wanted desperately to help me, but they just didn't know how. I couldn't blame them because I didn't know how either. My mom suggested that I visit a counselor, and my father told me he'd cover the cost.

Together, he and my mom prayed with me and asked God to help me in this difficult time. The next day, my life took an entirely new direction—and one step closer to discovering my Secret Name.

Rebekah knew her family's future was at stake and Jacob's life was in jeopardy. She cooked up one final plan, hoping to create some needed space between her two sons. She settled on forcing Jacob into exile.

> "Your brother Esau is consoling himself with the thought of killing you. Now then, my son, do what I say: Flee at once to my brother Laban in Haran. Stay with him for a while until your brother's fury subsides. When your brother is no longer angry with you and forgets what you did to him, I'll send

word for you to come back from there. Why should I lose both of you in one day?"

Genesis 27:42–45

Perhaps Rebekah was a little oblivious? Notice her words to Jacob:

"Until your brother's fury subsides?"

"When your brother is no longer angry?"

"When [he] . . . forgets what you did?"

Call me crazy, but I don't think Esau was about to dismiss Jacob's deception anytime soon.

So Rebekah concocted another quick fix solution. She said to Isaac, "I'm disgusted with living because of these Hittite women. If Jacob takes a wife from among the women of this land, from Hittite women like these, my life will not be worth living."

Cloaked in dramatic overtones, Rebekah's request was a backhanded attack on Esau's choice of a wife. Evidently unhappy with his intermarriage, she seized upon the present circumstances as an opportune time to verbalize her disgust.

Unable to see through the deceit, Isaac called his son Jacob to him and commanded him, "Do not marry a Canaanite woman. Go at once…to the house of your mother's father. Take a wife for yourself there, from among the daughters of Laban, your mother's brother."

Isaac prayed with Jacob and asked God to help him in this difficult time. "May God Almighty bless you and make you fruitful and increase your numbers until you become a community of peoples. May he give you and your descendants the blessing given to Abraham, so that you may take possession of the land where you now live as an alien, the land God gave to Abraham."

The next day, Jacob's life took an entirely new direction—and one step closer to discovering his Secret Name.

7

THREE HEARTBREAKS

My senior year in high school brought with it three major heartbreaks—significant enough I considered turning my back on God for good.

I didn't doubt his existence—I just doubted his presence in my life. God seemed uncaring and impotent and, either way, I figured I couldn't count on him.

Before those three trials, my life hummed along, and I was more than content to live my sheltered existence. Until then I never had to personalize my faith, so when the heartbreaks came, I nearly crumbled, no longer able to draw from my simple, yet untested, faith.

I wasn't struck by cancer or anything so dramatic. Sometimes it isn't the earth-shattering events that undo us, but rather a series of "random" incidents that chip away at us, piece by painful piece. As a high school kid, although ignorant of my Secret Name, I still believed I had some sense of identity, acceptance, and independence.

But, in a three-month period, God even took those illusions away.

THREE HEARTBREAKS

My Sense of Identity

Wrestling was my thing. Named cocaptain of my team, the coaches voted me the most valuable wrestler at several tournaments. In my final year of high school, I had my sights on medaling at the state level. Wrestling offered me an identity, and so, rather than blending in at my small high school, my accomplishments from the night before were heralded to everyone over the PA system during the morning announcements.

One night while driving my parents' car home from practice, only a few blocks away from my house outside Milwaukee, I approached a four-way stop sign. A car to my right idled with its lights on, hovering. Realizing the driver had the right-of-way, I remained behind my stop sign and waited.

Nothing.

I flickered my lights, signaling to the driver he could move through the intersection.

More nothing.

Eventually I pulled through the intersection and headed down the street, intending to turn in the alley behind my parents' house to park the car. I looked in my rearview mirror and noticed that the previously stationary car now followed me into the alley, its high beams blazing. As I tried to back into my parking spot, the car behind me blocked my way.

Frustrated, I opened my car door and got out. Two guys came out of the other car.

"What's your problem, punk?" the driver shouted.

"What are *you* talking about?" I shot back.

"At the stop sign back there . . . staring at us like that," he answered, now only about a foot away from my face.

"It was a four-way stop sign," I said. "I was waiting on you to move first."

"Yeah, well, don't do it again," he barked, glaring at me with hostility.

After a pregnant pause, having looked me up and down, he fired back to his accomplice, "Come on. Let's get out of here, man." With that he turned, giving me the impression he was headed back to his car.

I turned away as well—something I should have never done.

CRACK!

Unsure of whether I was struck by a fist, a headbutt, a pipe, or something else, I caught a crushing blow across the back of my head. Immediately, my vision went white, then black. I felt my legs buckle, and I hit the asphalt in a heap.

Car doors slammed and tires squealed. I struggled to stand. Tottering and stumbling, I felt rage fill every pore in my body. I scanned my vocabulary for something to shout, but no words came—only an angst-filled shriek. I kicked the car with a flash of fury, then staggered toward the house. I pushed the door open and fell to the floor. My mom immediately called an ambulance, then the police.

My concussion—confirmed by continuing headaches and short-term memory loss—kept me from wrestling in the state tournament that year. As a benched athlete watching my teammates compete in the last wrestling opportunity of my career, I found it difficult to lock onto any spiritual coordinates. Older people at church meant well, offering me warmed-over clichés like "Keep looking up" or "God has a plan."

All I knew was what I felt: this one must have slipped past God.

My Sense of Acceptance

Not long after the attack in the alley, I tried out for the school play. With my concussion healing, I didn't have to worry about getting hurt in play practice—or so I thought. We were staging *The Mouse That Roared*, and I was awarded a small part with only a few lines. Nonetheless, I embraced my part enthusiastically and looked forward to practice as a welcome break from the stress of classes.

On one ordinary afternoon, while rehearsing my lines with my fellow actors, I got tripped up. For some reason, my mind began to focus on the fact that I messed up. I knew my lines—that was never the problem—but the pressure to get them perfect mocked me. I settled for repeating self-condemning language in my head as a way of punishing myself for getting the words wrong.

Fast-forward twenty minutes. I was on stage doing my lines in real time before the entire cast. With my cue coming quickly, I felt anxiety creep up from my gut and into my throat. I knew what I needed to say and I knew how to say it, but no words came out.

I froze.

Memories of my childhood stuttering rushed in with a flood. The cast looked at me curiously, suspecting I might be joking. Several students chuckled, assuming I'd reciprocate the laugh or give up my charade and produce my anticipated lines in exchange.

All I produced was more awkward silence. Waves of embarrassment swept over me. I recognized that feeling. It's the same way I felt when my teacher called me out in front of my peers about the bunny in art class. Dejected, I walked off the stage in tears. I vowed never to go back.

I had more than a wounded ego. I was burdened by guilt too. Only weeks away from our first performance, I knew I let my friends down. Despite several gracious attempts by my director to get me to return to the cast, even offering me special exercises to overcome my anxiety, I firmly resisted. I followed through on quitting, the one thing I detested in others.

Over the years, I didn't have a shred of tolerance for those who joined the wrestling team and quit due to its grueling demands. Now in a different context, I was the one awarded a new Given Name—QUITTER. My small high school didn't find a place to hide the fact that the cocaptain of the wrestling team had been given a second beatdown—this time not by strangers in an alley, but by his own nerves on a stage.

It seemed like God was really losing his touch—but, lucky me, there was one more blow yet to come.

My Sense of Independence

Growing up, my family didn't have much money. So I was one of *those* eighteen-year-olds—the type that borrowed his parents' car and rode his bicycle the rest of the time.

Still, I loved my Trek mountain bike. I had an exaggerated affection for my bike and the accessories it touted: computer, shocks, pack, tire repair kit, water bottles, pump, and gel seat. My friend Kevin and I loved the thrill of trail riding—one season logging over two thousand miles as we mapped out most of greater Milwaukee. I would have gladly traded my bike in for a car, no matter how old or rusted, but money was hard to come by, so I made the best of my situation.

One day that spring, I rode my bike over to a friend's house in a fairly wealthy neighborhood. I parked it in my friend's garage and hung out for a couple of hours, sipping sodas in the living room. As the dinner hour approached, I stood to leave. For some reason, when heading out to the garage, I had a sick feeling come over me. When reaching for the doorknob, I expected my bike to be gone.

Call it a sixth sense. Call it dumb luck. Either way, my instincts were spot on. The bike was gone.

Sure it was only a missing bike, but not to me. I had reached my limit. Here I was, a senior in high school, trying to do the right things. I prayed before meals and read my Bible, at least sometimes, and what had all this hard work done for me?

THREE HEARTBREAKS

Absolutely nothing.

With these three strikes against me—my identity, acceptance, and independence stripped within a short period—I considered ditching the rules and the religion and going off on my own. After all, God ditched me, and nothing could convince me otherwise. Only an act of God could tilt the scale.

To my surprise God acted—and much sooner than I thought.

Stripped of *his* identity, acceptance, and independence, Jacob was expelled from home and forced to play the part of the wanderer. Not to mention his family was ripped in half and to top it off, he would never see his mother again.

Not too far into his journey, Jacob stopped to spend the night at an ordinary place. Night fell fast, and he settled for a certain piece of ground as a makeshift bed and a certain piece of stone as a makeshift pillow.

Feeling forsaken, Jacob desperately needed God to tilt the scale. The writer of Genesis explains how God acted despite Jacob's isolation:

> *He had a dream in which he saw a stairway resting on the earth, with its top reaching to heaven, and the angels of God were ascending and descending on it. There above it stood the Lord, and he said: "I am the Lord, the God of your father Abraham and the God of Isaac. I will give you and your descendants the land on which you are lying. Your descendants will be like the dust of the earth, and you will spread out to the west and to the east, to the north and to the south. All peoples on earth will be blessed through you and your offspring. I am with you and will watch over you wherever you go, and I will bring you back to this land. I will not leave you until I have done what I have promised you."*
>
> Genesis 28:12–15

At this point in Jacob's journey, God didn't presume Jacob had adopted him as his own. Instead, God seemed to go out of his way to distinguish himself as the God of his father Isaac and his grandfather Abraham. Not imposing at this point—minus the stairway and angelic vision—God wooed Jacob into a deeper relationship.

A child can only go so far walking in the footsteps of his father's faith. Evidently, God thought the time ripe for Jacob to begin taking his own steps. When God showed up, he didn't hit Jacob with a contract ("If you do this for me, then I'll do this for you"). He simply stated the facts. Then God unconditionally declared a refreshing stockpile of promises. With seven "I wills," he lavished a rather benevolent affirmation, independent of Jacob's performance:

1. I will give your descendants the land you are lying on.

2. Your descendants will be like the dust of the earth.

3. You will spread out to the west and to the east, the north and the south.

4. All peoples on earth will be blessed through your offspring.

5. I am with you and will watch over you wherever you go.

6. I will bring you back to the land.

7. I will not leave you until I have done what I promised.

Imagine you're Jacob. What do you do with this new knowledge? Unmarried and not even dating at the moment, you're told your babies are going to inherit the land you're presently lying on? (And you didn't even see a "for sale" sign the night before.) To top it off, God just vowed not to leave you until everything played out in real time.

In a matter of minutes, Jacob went from schemer to dreamer. He had been given a glimpse of his Secret Name even though he wouldn't inherit that new name for quite some time.

This tends to be the pattern. We get a tiny peek at *what could be*—the possible—while taking a vacation from *what is*—the actual. Only a fleeting foretaste, and then, as quick as it came, it's gone. The following days, years, and perhaps even decades help us hone in on that original vision we received. Time brings clarity. Yet for the moment we must be content to simply understand where we are and how far we must travel in order to arrive at our destination.

God presents our Secret Name in snippets for fear of information overload. The more we envision our new name, the more we want it. The hope is such a glance, however brief, will inspire us to get on the path of discovering who we were created to be.

In Jacob's case, he witnessed—if only for an instant—life was bigger than the little game of charades he played back home. Jolted, this epic reality frightened him.

Fortunately, it also fueled him.

> *When Jacob awoke from his sleep, he thought, "Surely the Lord is in this place, and I was not aware of it." He was afraid and said, "How awesome is this place! This is none other than the house of God; this is the gate of heaven."*
>
> Genesis 28:16–17

Sometimes we need to dream in order to wake up. Sometimes we must fall asleep in order to snap out of our slumber.

Jacob awoke a new man, or at least a man with a new perspective. "Early the next morning Jacob took the stone he had placed under his head and set it up as a pillar and poured oil on top of it. He called that place Bethel, though the city used to be called Luz."

God showed up, and even though Jacob hadn't fully received his Secret Name, he understood that his Given Names were not the summation of his earthly existence.

Like most humans, Jacob wanted to memorialize his otherworldly experience. In making his stone pillow into an altar, he solidified his dream, pulling it from the heavens and lashing it to the earth. Perhaps sensing his own name change in the future, Jacob desired to rename something in the present, and so he called his place of encounter Bethel, meaning "the house of God."

For years to come, the stone altar would stand as a memorial to Jacob and his descendants as the place where the natural and the supernatural converged.

At the age of eighteen, immediately after my three heartbreaks, I also witnessed a convergence of the natural and the supernatural. And just like in Jacob's experience, God sent me a special messenger. Hardly angelic, my visitor nevertheless brought me a unique message, informing me that I was more than my Given Names. Although UNKNOWN to myself, I was apparently known to God.

My messenger informed me that God not only knew my Secret Name, but he was ready for me to discover that name and, in the process, embrace my future.

PART
THREE
Embracing the Future

*Our mistake lies not in the intensity
of our desire for happiness,
but in the weakness of it.*

—John Piper

8
GRACE INTERRUPTED

Unlike Jacob's experience, God never showed up in my dreams. Fortunately for me, God whispers in more ways than one.

Following my three heartbreaks, depression invaded my space, pressing in without even asking my permission. I had lost my sense of identity, acceptance, and independence, and as a result, I felt like I'd lost God—or maybe that he just lost me somewhere along the way.

I figured God cared about important people like presidents and popes and important things like global warming and the global market—but I couldn't fathom how a boy with a girl's name showed up on his radar.

Swallowing the lie—that I didn't matter much—seemed easier. How could my recent experiences harmonize with God's preordained plan?

Such simplistic logic seemed safer because the moment I counted for more than skin and bones was the moment I had to interface with dangerous soul issues like beauty, honor, bravery, and value. Much easier to march under the banner of "purposeless existence layered with random chance."

Funny how we humans go to great lengths to do life in our own strength. After all, if we abandon God first, then he can't abandon us. Like a middle school crush that can't bear the thought of rejection, we extinguish our new "flame" before that "flame" has the chance to extinguish us. We prefer self-induced loneliness over other-initiated rejection. With the former, we're at the steering wheel, in control. But with the latter, we're sticking our necks out, and we'd much rather play it safe.

All our baggage makes it hard for us to move, so it's a good thing God isn't waiting on us. God already made the first move. It's called creation, and it's only one of the ways he woos our hearts back to him—through brilliant colored skyscapes suspended effortlessly in the air. Through brash, mighty waterfalls crashing boldly over cliffs. Through gentle breezes blowing sweet smells inherent of shifting seasons. His beauty whispers loudly.

But God also moved through his Son Jesus. In him we see God's compassion, love, forgiveness, and grace. Jesus said, "Anyone who has seen me has seen the Father." The author of Hebrews develops that theme further.

> *"In the past God spoke to our forefathers through the prophets at many times and in various ways, but in these last days he has spoken to us by his Son, whom he appointed heir of all things, and through whom he made the universe. The Son is the radiance of God's glory and the exact representation of his being, sustaining all things by his powerful word. After he had provided purification for sins, he sat down at the right hand of the Majesty in heaven."*
>
> *Hebrews 1:1–3*

Make no mistake, God has spoken. The real question is, have we listened?

Ironically, we tend to hear best amidst personal heartbreak. Maybe God speaks louder in such scenarios. Or maybe we just listen closer.

After school one afternoon, I hopped into my parents' vehicle for the half-hour trip home. Dad passed me a rather plain-looking white envelope with my name handwritten across the front.

"What's this?" I asked.

"I'm not sure. Your mother gave it to me."

I carelessly tore open the envelope and clumsily unfolded the somewhat rigid stationery. To my surprise, inside were a few pages of lined paper—and some cold hard cash! I counted the stack of bills and then turned to the letter, intrigued with the anonymous author.

> *Kary,*
>
> *You don't know me or my wife and I must admit, I don't normally write letters to strangers, but something rather strange happened to me the other day. You see your mom works with my wife JoAnne at Marshall's. She was telling JoAnne about how you went through a series of trials lately: the stolen bike and the assault in the alley.*
>
> *JoAnne relayed your story to me over dinner the other day. Kary, I'm telling you God spoke to me. In that moment he told me with unmistakable clarity, "Carl you need to encourage this young man." In my whole life God never told me anything that clearly. I shook it off at first, but then the message came back even stronger, "Carl, I can't afford to have Kary discouraged. I need him and you need to encourage him."*
>
> *I knew I had to listen. So I am giving you this money in order for you to buy a new bike. I am convinced that God has great plans for you. Don't ever doubt this and don't be discouraged.*
>
> *God needs you, Kary!*
> *Carl Muenzmaier*

Perplexed, I looked up from the letter, struggling to quantify my unbelief. "God needs *me*?" I whispered—half mocking, but also half hoping.

Moments before I had questioned if God even knew I existed, and now a stranger just informed me that God couldn't afford to have me discouraged? A large part of me didn't want to accept what I had just read—I couldn't take another disappointment or broken dream.

Still, I couldn't shake it. God had just shown up and given me a significant message.

And I wondered—what if that message was *true*?

Up until Jacob's dream, God was someone he only knew from afar. Then all of a sudden, God showed up with a message, promising him seven gifts in the form of seven "I will" statements.

Right after God's unconditional promises were heaped high upon his future—ranging from descendants to land—Jacob responded with his own promises wrapped in performance.

He couldn't deal with "Grace," so he quickly interrupted her, shifting the mood and slanting the entire supernatural experience into one big business transaction.

> *Then Jacob made a vow, saying, "If God will be with me and will watch over me on this journey I am taking and will give me food to eat and clothes to wear so that I return safely to my father's house, then the Lord will be my God and this stone that I have set up as a pillar will be God's house, and of all that you give me I will give you a tenth."*
>
> Genesis 28:20–22

Jacob rained on Grace's parade by promising to pay her off if she came through. And while on the subject, Jacob promised a lousy payoff. What could he possibly give God that he didn't already own?

Jacob was in no position to bargain, either. Remember, he had a cold stone in place of a pillow and a fat zero in place of a wallet. Unemployed at the moment, how could he give God a tenth of anything? Old patterns are hard to break, however, and Jacob's reply revealed that he was still miles away from receiving his Secret Name.

Jacob—unwilling to abandon his wheeling-and-dealing posture, even with someone as impressive as God—needed a lesson in economic etiquette. Thankfully, God didn't allow Jacob to pay off Grace.

Up until then, I only knew God from afar, but overnight, God now had my attention.

Shortly after receiving Carl's letter, I drove through downtown Milwaukee, parked the car, grabbed my Bible and my journal, and headed to the large white rocks that outlined the lakeshore. If God had any intention of additional information, I now sat poised and ready to hear him.

Propped up on the rocks, I made a makeshift altar—my attention fully directed to the Bible and the strange letter from the strange man spread out before me. With a somewhat bustling pace, I turned the crinkly pages of Scripture, hoping for more clarity. After a few minutes, I stumbled upon a portion from a prophet named Jeremiah. Evidently, he wanted to remind his readers that God hadn't forgotten them or their situation.

His inspirational ideas seemed consistent with Carl's letter. Excitedly, my eyes scanned both documents at a hurried pace, picking up on a unique pattern. Replacing my heartbreaks with hope, promises suddenly popped off the pages:

1. I can't afford to have you discouraged.

2. I need you.

3. I have big plans for you.

4. "You will call upon me and come and pray to me, and I will listen to you."[1]

5. "You will seek me and find me when you seek me with all your heart."[2]

6. "I will be found by you," declares the Lord, "and will bring you back from captivity."[3]

7. "I will gather you from all the nations and places where I have banished you," declares the Lord, "and will bring you back to the place from which I carried you into exile."[4]

Although intrigued, I was unsure of how to respond to the seven gifts in the form of the seven "I will" statements strewn out before me. With God's unconditional promises heaped high upon my future—ranging from plans to prophecies—I responded with my own promises wrapped in performance.

I told God that if he came through, I'd spend the summer after my senior year as a counselor at a camp. I also vowed to give up any hopes of a wrestling gig in college and head instead to a Bible institute. I even professed a willingness to serve as an overseas missionary in the deepest jungle in New Guinea.

I couldn't deal with Grace either, so I quickly interrupted her, shifting the mood and slanting the entire supernatural experience into one big business transaction. I promised to do my part if God did his. Just like Jacob's response, mine revealed that I too was miles away from receiving my Secret Name.

9
MIRRORS TELL HALF-TRUTHS

Homiletics class at Bible Institute—the required and dreaded course which cruelly exposed one's speaking flaws and then (hopefully) honed one's preaching skills—was barreling toward me like a raging bull, and my fear of public speaking the ill-fated red flag.

Still haunted by the demons that bit me during high school play practice the year before, the last thing I wanted to do was showcase my ineffectiveness. Even though I aspired to find my voice and express my inner thoughts, I feared the required risk.

On my way to class, I stopped at my mailbox and found an unexpected letter: "Kary M. Oberbrunner, please come to the address listed below in order to pick up your file. Failure to do so before 30 days from now will result in your file being promptly destroyed."

All during class I obsessed about this mysterious file and its contents. As soon as my schedule opened up, I hopped onto my new bicycle—thanks, Carl!—and rode across town to the given address. Upon producing my perplexing letter to the receptionist, I was handed a rather thick manila folder with a red tab across the top that read: "Speech—Oberbrunner, Kary (m) 76."

This folder contained the full story of my time in and out of speech therapy, beginning when I was just six years old. In spite of forgetting this chapter of my life, even if I *had* remembered, reading the detailed account from the speech therapist's point of view added some much-needed color to the distant, gray memory.

On the first page I read:

Referral date: 8-20-83
Kary has a learning disability. The disability is a handicap.
The type: Speech/Language

The session notes stunned me. I had no idea my speech problem was so severe.

Kary has difficulty talking with adults and peers in situations. He seems to accept his speech difficulty, but is embarrassed by it. Mrs. Oberbrunner has noticed the problem since Kary was two years old. He is beginning to hit his leg as a way to get his speech going. He appears to be bothered by his lack of fluency of speech. He has stated that he is afraid he won't be liked because of it. A disability in learning appears to exist at this time with the probability of a much greater disability. The analysis of functioning indicates that Kary has a functioning condition as per Wis. Stats 115.76.

A language sample was transcribed and analyzed to illustrate the severity of the impediment.

One hundred percent of the utterances contained interjections of "um" with at least one repetition. For example: "Then um then um then the um um um then um then the hippopotamus um um um um is walking by a fruit stand um then um then she took the bottom then then crashed then um then um and then she said, 'oops.'" Toward the end of the session, Kary appeared to give up after a couple of difficult utterances. His voice trailed off in mid-sentence.

Serving as an uninvited truth teller, this manila folder reflected my past with fresh eyes, mirroring my present struggles with entirely new hues. After all, I still had homiletics class to contend with, and soon enough I'd have to stand before my peers and deliver another speech.

As I read my folder, one childhood detail emerged with brand-new clarity. I remembered my mom sitting by my bedside at night reading me a prophecy from the book of Isaiah: "The stammering tongue will be fluent and clear." Whenever I was in tears, swept up in emotional overload, Mom stayed optimistic—firmly convinced that God would heal my tongue and use me in a mighty manner.

Still believing that promise—now a young man caught up in the throes of bleak circumstances—my mother's belief in prophecy was the only thing that kept me going long after logic had left the building.

She couldn't help it; whenever Rebekah looked at her son Jacob, she saw him through the eyes of the prophecy. She couldn't help it; God gave Rebekah an unbelievable promise, months before her two boys even drew breath.

> *The Lord said to [Rebekah], "Two nations are in your womb, and two -peoples from within you will be separated; one -people will be stronger than the other, and the older will serve the younger."*
>
> Genesis 25:23

Most likely, Jacob mentally rehearsed this prophecy while wandering in the wilderness, headed toward a relative he'd never met, banished from family and friends. Soon enough, he stumbled upon a band of shepherds at a common watering hole. After some formal greetings, Jacob inquired if they knew his uncle Laban. Providentially, they did and, a split second later, Laban's daughter, a shepherdess named Rachel, arrived to water her father's sheep.

Not skipping a beat, Jacob sprang into action and watered all the sheep for her. Unable to control his emotions, he wept and kissed Rachel, informing her that he was a relative, at which point Rachel sprinted home to tell her father, Laban.

> As soon as Laban heard the news about Jacob, his sister's son, he hurried to meet him. He embraced him and kissed him and brought him to his home, and there Jacob told him all these things. Then Laban said to him, "You are my own flesh and blood." After Jacob had stayed with him for a whole month, Laban said to him, "Just because you are a relative of mine, should you work for me for nothing? Tell me what your wages should be."
>
> Genesis 29:13–15

After a month of working for Laban, his uncle finally caught the hint. Rather than settling on a specified salary, Jacob desired something much more valuable. More properly put, *someone* much more valuable. He knew he couldn't pay the required bride price required for Rachel, so instead, he negotiated seven years of service for her hand in marriage.

> Now Laban had two daughters; the name of the older was Leah, and the name of the younger was Rachel. Leah had weak eyes, but Rachel was lovely in form, and beautiful. Jacob was in love with Rachel and said, "I'll work for you seven years in return for your younger daughter Rachel." Laban said, "It's better that I give her to you than to some other man. Stay here with me." So Jacob served seven years

MIRRORS TELL HALF-TRUTHS

to get Rachel, but they seemed like only a few days to him because of his love for her.

Genesis 29:16–20

Time passed rather quickly, and the day came for Jacob and Rachel to marry and consummate their relationship. Unfortunately, a scandal loomed over the festivities, slipping past everyone—including Jacob.

When evening came, he took his daughter Leah and gave her to Jacob, and Jacob lay with her... When morning came, there was Leah! So Jacob said to Laban, "What is this you have done to me? I served you for Rachel, didn't I? Why have you deceived me?"

Genesis 29:23, 25

With the deceiver now deceived, the atmosphere wasn't exactly inviting. But rather than apologizing, Laban offered excuses and then—in exchange for seven more years of service—another daughter.

Laban replied, "It is not our custom here to give the younger daughter in marriage before the older one. Finish this daughter's bridal week; then we will give you the younger one also, in return for another seven years of work." And Jacob did so. He finished the week with Leah, and then Laban gave him his daughter Rachel to be his wife.

Genesis 29:26–28

Only a short time before, Jacob, the younger sibling, followed his mother's orders as a means of acquiring his older brother's blessing. Now Leah, the older sibling, followed her father's orders as a means of acquiring her younger sister's husband. On the receiving end, forced to drink a little of his own medicine, Jacob didn't enjoy the aftertaste. He gave Laban an ultimatum.

> *"Send me on my way so I can go back to my own homeland. Give me my wives and children, for whom I have served you, and I will be on my way. You know how much work I've done for you." But Laban said to him, "If I have found favor in your eyes, please stay. I have learned by divination that the Lord has blessed me because of you." He added, "Name your wages, and I will pay them."*
>
> Genesis 30:25–28

Serving as an uninvited truth teller, Laban's treachery reflected Jacob's past with fresh eyes, mirroring his present struggles with entirely new hues. After all, he still had Esau to contend with, and soon enough he'd have to stand before his brother and deliver another apology.

As an older man caught up in the throes of bleak circumstances, his mother's belief in prophecy was now the only thing that kept him going long after logic had left the building.

I sat on the curb, flipping through the manila folder, wondering. Was I simply a product of my disorder? Would it control my adult life? Suddenly a few pages stapled together toward the end caught my eye.

> *Notice of the Multidisciplinary Team Findings Date: 2/18/85 Kary doesn't have a disability or a handicap.*

Poring over the session notes, I was stunned. I had no idea my speech problem was cured in such a dramatic—even miraculous—fashion. My mother's prophecy was well on its way to coming true.

Kary has been enrolled in speech therapy since November 1983, when his parents were concerned with his stuttering in his expressive language. Kary has made remarkable progress to date. Parent, teacher, and clinician no longer see any evidence of stuttering behavior. Analysis of current functioning suggests that Kary does not have a handicapping condition as identified as speech and language. Recommendations: Dismiss from Speech Classes

That Given Name—STUTTERER—wouldn't define my destiny after all. God had a different name in mind, and I no longer felt mastered by that disability—not that it made the preaching class easier!

Progress was possible, and prophecy too. I reflected and rested again on the verse that meant so much to my mother: "The stammering tongue will be fluent and clear."

While Jacob labored under Laban, the DECEIVER, his destiny unraveled at a lethargic pace. Working for a boss without integrity offered its fair share of emotional abuse. Unfortunately, back then no labor union rushed to his defense. Thankfully, Jacob had a Divine Advocate watching his back.

God made good on his original prophecy to Rebekah concerning her son Jacob ("One people will be stronger than the other, and the older will serve the younger"), and as the days piled high, so did Jacob's economic worth.

The weak animals went to Laban and the strong ones to Jacob. In this way [Jacob] grew exceedingly prosperous and came to own large flocks, and maidservants and menservants, and camels and donkeys.

Genesis 30:42–43

Although blessed by God, Jacob still lived in light of his Given Name—SCHEMER. His shady operational overtones, manifested through a manipulative breeding strategy of his flocks, demonstrated that he was still in desperate need of a new identity.

Jacob's quest was far from over. His Secret Name was still, for the moment, a secret. Yet he was beginning to sink his teeth into a future that looked entirely different. Mirrors reflect a shade of reality, but in the end they have their limitations too. Turns out, mirrors might only tell half-truths after all.

10

PACKING YOUR SUITCASE

Exile is temporary. Secret Names are forever.
For Jacob, these facts felt like fantasy until one ordinary day when God showed up and told Jacob to pack up and "go back to the land of your fathers and to your relatives, and I will be with you."

Apparently, Jacob had learned all he could within his current circumstances, and now it was time to move on. He sent word to his wives, Rachel and Leah, "to come out to the fields where his flocks were. He said to them, 'I see that your father's attitude toward me is not what it was before, but the God of my father has been with me. You know that I've worked for your father with all my strength, yet your father has cheated me by changing my wages ten times. However, God has not allowed him to harm me.' "

Over the years, Jacob exerted tremendous energy trying to stay positive despite working for an unethical boss. With Jacob's situation in mind, we might wonder why God allows his children to remain in painful places.

One answer is that times of testing instill character development. Pain doesn't have to be purposeless. While enduring Laban's treachery, Jacob learned much about himself, his sin, and his need to make things right with his older brother, Esau.

God puts "Labans" in our lives for a reason. Our blind spots suddenly come into sharp focus as we witness the same shortcomings in others. Jacob saw his own unhealthy tendencies with fresh eyes as Laban dealt deceit his way over a twenty-year span. I'm betting Jacob somehow found a sympathetic spot in his heart for Esau.

Don't be too impressed, though. Jacob hadn't discovered his Secret Name yet, and residues of less than ideal labels still clung to him.

When God finally gave him the go-ahead, Jacob put his children and his wives on camels, but rather than facing Laban, he snuck away quietly. When on autopilot, he still operated in light of his other Given Name—DECEIVER. Three days later, however, someone broke the news to Laban. Taking his relatives with him, Laban pursued Jacob for seven days and caught up with him in the hill country of Gilead.

Against his will, Jacob would have to confront Laban and, in the process, any fragments of his Given Names that remained.

Even though fear hijacked me a time or two during my homiletics class, I lived to tell about it.

Finally beginning to find my voice, I had a bunch of emotions brewing on the inside, and, in addition to speaking, I fancied writing as another venue of self-expression. Many times I even preferred the pen over the pulpit, realizing an audience of paper has a few advantages over one of people, like a concept called editing. I wrote in my journal constantly, even occasionally submitting an essay or poem to a magazine.

More and more speaking opportunities came my way. My courage grew with each talk, and I witnessed my Given Name—in this case my SPEECH IMPEDIMENT—fade over time.

As I neared the end of my two-year stint at the Bible

Institute, I had a desire to get more education. I thought maybe college would prepare me for my next step, whatever that step was. In the midst of my decision-making, I stopped in to see Jim Corbett a local disc jockey I had befriended.

Intimidated by the cost of school, I felt convicted not to take out any loans. I knew there was no way I could come up with the tens of thousands of dollars needed to complete a debt-free college and graduate school stint, but I couldn't shake the feeling.

I visited Jim, hoping for some sort of sign, even confirmation perhaps, for the next phase of my convoluted journey. Then again, we had only planned coffee. What transforming thing ever resulted from caffeine and chatting?

Although I've forgotten most of what took place during my afternoon with Jim, he gave me two gifts I still remember: $500 in cash and a Bible reference.

On that particular day, the $500 meant much more to me than the reference. In a world of bills, money speaks loudly, especially to a poor kid heading off to college. Although I didn't think $500 would do much, I took this unsolicited gift as a sign that God might provide for my needs both now and in the future.

As I prepared to leave, Jim stopped me. "Kary," he said tenderly, "hold on one moment." He grabbed a piece of scrap paper and a pen from a junk drawer.

"Here, I think the Father wants you to have this." He said it in almost a whisper.

"Thanks," I replied with uncertainty, glancing down and noticing "GALATIANS 5:1" in capital letters across the paper.

I folded the small scrap, placed it in my pocket, and headed out the door, not thinking about it or Jim again for quite some time. It wasn't until years later that it came crashing back into my world, ironically, on the day I discovered my Secret Name.

When Laban showed up, he was a bit perturbed—chasing down your son-in-law and daughters across rough terrain tends to have that effect. But then again, Jacob wasn't in good spirits either.

> *"What is my crime?" [Jacob] asked Laban. "What sin have I committed that you hunt me down?... I have been with you for twenty years now.... The heat consumed me in the daytime and the cold at night, and sleep fled from my eyes. It was like this for the twenty years I was in your household. I worked for you fourteen years for your two daughters and six years for your flocks, and you changed my wages ten times."*
> Genesis 31:36, 38, 40–41

Thankfully, God hadn't forgotten Jacob. Remember the whole ladder from heaven vision? From that day twenty years before until that moment, God had observed every injustice—and Jacob knew it.

He told Laban, "If the God of my father, the God of Abraham and the Fear of Isaac, had not been with me, you would surely have sent me away empty-handed. But God has seen my hardship and the toil of my hands, and last night he rebuked you."

Unimpressed with Jacob's speech, Laban shared events from his perspective:

> *"The women are my daughters, the children are my children, and the flocks are my flocks. All you see is mine. Yet what can I do today about these daughters of mine, or about the children they have borne?"*
> Genesis 31:43

Despite Laban's warped view, he knew he couldn't hang on to them. He knew Jacob stayed as long as he could, and the only thing left undone was the goodbye. Laban suggested they make a covenant as a symbol of their decision to separate. Jacob agreed.

> *So Jacob took a stone and set it up as a pillar. He said to his relatives, "Gather some stones." So they took stones and piled them in a heap, and they ate there by the heap. . . . It was also called Mizpah, because [Laban] said, "May the Lord keep watch between you and me when we are away from each other." Jacob took an oath in the name of the [God] of his father Isaac. He offered a sacrifice there in the hill country and invited his relatives to a meal. After they had eaten, they spent the night there. Early the next morning Laban kissed his grandchildren and his daughters and blessed them. Then he left and returned home.*
> Genesis 31:45–46, 49, 53–55

Jacob headed out in a different direction—one that included a run-in with an uninvited guest.

11

IN THE CAMP OF ANGELS

I entered the "Hoosier" state feeling like a stranger and quite unsure of what a "Hoosier" actually was. (To this day I'm still confused.)

During my first month at college, the tuition costs nearly gave me ulcers. Reflecting on my monthly statements, I slowly opened the door for fear to creep in. Unclear of my options, I conducted a little inventory on my assets. Knowing I didn't have too much to offer, but also feeling an increasing desire to write, I decided to schedule a meeting with the president of the college, Dr. Ron Manahan.

After borrowing a suit from some guy in my hall and asking God to give me favor, I walked across campus and into the president's office. I introduced myself and explained the dilemma—I had a passion to express myself through writing and also an inability to pay for my college and seminary bills.

For forty-five minutes, in painstaking detail, I talked about my "brilliant" idea. I hoped the college would publish the book I wanted to write and then enjoy the full profits as means of payment for my tuition costs. (Looking back I'm more than a little embarrassed at my zeal.)

President Manahan, an overly humble and generous man, graciously listened to every word that flowed out of my naive mouth. He smiled and nodded. He asked polite questions, and at the end of my spiel, he regretfully explained the impossibility of my request. He suggested I contact a gentleman by the name of Max Anders, a local alumnus and prolific writer. Dr. Manahan thought Max might be able to help me in my quest to be a writer, providing some unique insight and much-needed encouragement.

Following his sincere prayer for my situation and me, I left the president's office discouraged, but not defeated. I knew something would eventually break. Little did I know it would be me.

After Jacob's run-in with Laban, he continued on his journey, obedient to God's instruction to go back to his native land. He must have feared what lay ahead of him. The last time he saw his brother Esau, he was fleeing for his life.

Had time healed Esau's wounds, or was he still intent on exterminating Jacob's hope of a Secret Name and his next breath? With destiny directing him, he'd soon find out.

True to his word, God kept tabs on Jacob, providing angel escorts along the way.

> *The angels of God met him. When Jacob saw them, he said, "This is the camp of God!" So he named that place Mahanaim. Jacob sent messengers ahead of him to his brother Esau in the land of Seir, the country of Edom. He instructed them: "This is what you are to say to my master Esau: 'Your servant Jacob says, I have been staying with Laban and have remained there till now. I have cattle and donkeys, sheep and goats, menservants and maidservants. Now I am sending this message to my lord, that I may find favor in your eyes.'"*
>
> Genesis 32:1–5

Hoping to escape his Given Name for good, Jacob desired to mend the rocky relationship with Esau—the brother he swindled, impersonated, and supplanted. When the messengers returned to Jacob, they said, "We went to your brother Esau, and now he is coming to meet you, and four hundred men are with him."

Four hundred men?

You don't dispatch this many men if you just have a friendly drink in mind with your kid brother.

Maybe time wasn't an ally after all. In great fear and distress, Jacob divided those who were with him into two groups, and the flocks and herds and camels as well. Instead of equal treatment, he played favorites and protected his preferred people and possessions just in case God didn't stand behind his word and deliver him from Esau. He figured, "If Esau comes and attacks one group, the group that is left may escape."

Looks like his Given Name still defined him because the consummate schemer drafted a backup plan to outmaneuver his brother's fury just in case Esau outmaneuvered God's watchful eye.

Jacob's actions revealed the duplicity within his heart. Although he knew God's prophecy about protecting his loved ones and his livelihood, at the present moment, he was a bit overwhelmed. But rather than just manipulating circumstances as in the past, he also vented via prayer about his impending future.

> *"O God of my father Abraham, God of my father Isaac, O Lord, who said to me, 'Go back to your country and your relatives, and I will make you prosper,' I am unworthy of all the kindness and faithfulness you have shown your servant. I had only my staff when I crossed this Jordan, but now I have become two groups. Save me, I pray, from the hand of my brother Esau, for I am afraid he will come and attack me, and also the mothers with their children."*
>
> Genesis 32:9–11

Jacob's conversation with God helped his own morale, reminding him of God's promises—promises that he'd succeed and promises that a Secret Name lay in the cards for him. Jacob continued to remind both God and himself, saying, "You have said, 'I will surely make you prosper and will make your descendants like the sand of the sea, which cannot be counted.'"

Jacob left Laban because God instructed him, but at the moment, on the eve of a potentially violent reunion with Esau, he probably saw himself as a simple pawn in God's cosmic game of chess.

Although Jacob felt alone, vulnerable, and confused, he knew his Secret Name was closer than ever. Jacob named this present location Mahanaim—"Two Camps"—a name that paralleled the two camps (faith and fear), which defined his heart and the two names (his Given One and his Secret One) that fought for his attention. Soon enough he'd find out which name would define his destiny.

I eventually connected with that local author Max Anders. He agreed to critique some of my work.

Writing had become my lifeline, a venue in which I could express my thoughts and emotions. But my writing seemed forced, not fluid. The pieces I penned tasted bland, sprinkled with unoriginal clichés. Every piece I wrote subconsciously passed through a type of filter—ensuring my words were free of toxins like tension, fear, and unbridled emotion.

I wrote to please the critic in my head rather than the sojourner in my soul. I wanted my readers to think well of me by not seeing my struggle. I believed the lie that not only the Message needed to be spotless, but also the messenger.

The rare time I wrote without my internal judge accusing me I'd cross it out or rip it up, fearing that someone might read it and think less of me.

Although Max Anders tolerated my writing, he offered a few critiques. "Your work still needs the burnish that only comes from time and trials, but that will come." He told me to be patient. Although that wasn't exactly what I wanted to hear, it was better than what he could have said.

I desperately wanted someone to declare me worthy of writing a story. Little did I know that God was writing a story within me—at his own pace and in his own way.

Looking out my dorm window on those autumn afternoons, I couldn't help noticing the surrounding landscape lacked the lush cornfields promised in the glossy photographs from my college catalog. Instead, I saw only desolate deserts outlined in financial stress and relational strain. God wasn't leading me into green pastures by the most direct path.

One of the main reasons I chose this college was to join my girlfriend of three years. She was starting as a freshman, and I would be a transfer in as a junior. Without warning, relatively early on in the semester, she informed me while on a date that we were done.

Since nothing seemed to be "working out" the way I'd pictured, I started to doubt my ability to interpret God's voice. I felt foolish, vulnerable, and confused. Blowing through more than $7,000 in tuition expenses and a three-year relationship in a matter of months left me shell-shocked.

I searched for confirmation that I was on the right path. Staying in Indiana added to my fair share of failure and embarrassment, and at the moment, I had more than I had asked for.

I vowed never to stick my neck out again—not for God or for anyone else. So on a cold December evening, before packing up for the semester and maybe for good, I had my own "dark night of the soul." I reached the end of my patience and my checking account.

I knelt in my dorm room with a few of my close friends, desperately asking God to show up with a sign. We prayed for a clear answer, and I negotiated a plan. Either God would give me $7,500 in the next four weeks over Christmas break for the second semester, or I would come back in January with boxes to pack up my belongings and my hope of a better life.

Three days before the semester started back up again, there was no money in sight. Late one evening, I was sulking in my parents' living room, assuming life as I knew it was now over. In a matter of hours, I would withdraw from the college.

Dad came downstairs and inquired what my plans were. "Well, no money came in," I said callously. "So I guess God doesn't want me to go back to school."

My dad looked at me tenderly and said, "Kary, is this a financial problem or a spiritual problem?"

Backpedaling, I searched for an excuse. "I don't understand," I said. "What do you mean?"

"Since when do you let your bank account balance dictate God's will for your life?" he suggested. "Maybe you're not willing to walk in faith and trust him. Remember, faith means that unless God shows up, you'll fail."

"But I don't want to fail," I shot back bitterly. "I'm not going to trust God ever again if it means failure."

My reply rang loud and clear—reverberating off the walls, then sinking back into my soul. His question stuck with me the next three days. I tried to shake it, but as much as I didn't want to admit it, he was right. I had shut off my heart to God because of the pain I believed he caused me.

I spent a number of hours venting my anger at God. As I did, the pain subsided, and the less pain I felt, the more trust followed. My prayers shifted from "show me the cash" to "show me your will." The more I opened up my heart to God, the more I knew he wanted me to return, serve as a student chaplain, and remain debt free. I committed to go back for the second semester and attend as long as my bills were paid.

That January I *went back* and *never looked back*, eventually completing a bachelor's and a master's degree debt free. Unexplainably, I never once needed to take out loans for my education. Although I always held at least one job throughout my time as a student, the amount of revenue I earned never came close to covering the cost of living, school, and books. Often when picking up the mail from my box, I'd find a pile of money wrapped in a piece of notebook paper with a Bible verse scribbled on it, reminding me that God hadn't forgotten me.

These completely anonymous donations convinced me that somehow God must have placed angels around me. The monetary gifts usually came at the very last moment, but they were never late.

Deeply humbled by God's faithfulness, at the age of twenty-one I committed to live a life of faith, never again allowing finances to limit his leading in my life.

Jacob had his own dark night of the soul. He knew that unless God showed up, Esau could have his head on a platter by morning. This reality caused Jacob to wear one of his Given Names—SCHEMER—one more time.

Although Jacob communicated with God, he also conspired with others. He looked at his bank account balance, measured in terms of sheep, goats, camels, cows, bulls, and donkeys, and rationalized what he could part with and still survive. Although God had other things in mind—miracles!—Jacob never bothered to entertain these thoughts. He wanted to walk by sight and not by faith.

> *[Jacob] selected a gift for his brother Esau: two hundred female goats and twenty male goats, two hundred ewes and twenty rams, thirty female camels with their young, forty cows and ten bulls, and twenty female donkeys and ten male donkeys. He put them in the care of his servants, each herd by itself, and said to his servants, "Go ahead of me, and keep some space between the herds."*

IN THE CAMP OF ANGELS

He instructed the one in the lead: "When my brother Esau meets you and asks, 'To whom do you belong, and where are you going, and who owns all these animals in front of you?' then you are to say, 'They belong to your servant Jacob. They are a gift sent to my lord Esau, and he is coming behind us.'"

He also instructed the second, the third and all the others who followed the herds: "You are to say the same thing to Esau when you meet him."

Genesis 32:13–19

Jacob's logic was simple—protect himself at all costs. He tried once again to carve out his Secret Name. But instead, he simply embodied his Given Names. The Scriptures lift the hood up on Jacob's thought process, "I will pacify him with these gifts I am sending on ahead; later, when I see him, perhaps he will receive me."

Rather than stepping boldly into his divine destiny, he tried to sneak in the back door. But as he quickly found out, the back door is always graciously locked. We can only enter through center stage.

This type of grand entrance is the only way God gets glory, and it's the only way we get our Secret Name.

PART FOUR

Your Secret Name

*The nations will see your righteousness,
and all kings your glory;
you will be called by a new name
that the mouth of the Lord will bestow.*

—Isaiah 62:2

12

PUSHING THROUGH THE PAST

I passed class after class, completing my undergraduate degree with my sights set on seminary, then the Air Force as a military chaplain.

Although life hummed by, I noticed an underlying trend. My outlook evolved from carefree and happy to reserved and troubled. On the exterior, I appeared pleasant and unattached, but on the inside I felt distracted and conflicted.

Relationally, I grew distant. I erected invisible barriers that kept others at arm's length—just the way I wanted. At the time I didn't understand. Reflecting back, I know why I insisted on relational space. I feared pain.

In the past, relationships sprang up and hurt me. I wasn't about to leave myself unguarded again. The sudden death of both grandparents and the near death of my brother from his drug overdose had caused me to flip off a very significant switch—my emotions.

As a result, I carried an increasing amount of strain into my relationships. In one sense I loved them because they gave me value and worth.

But I also asked too much of them. I believed they had the power to break me. Naturally, relationships were a source of pain, and investing value or emotion in them only increased their power to harm me. So in this sense I hated them because they revealed my lack of control over my life. This internal conflict kept me vulnerable and fragile.

I hid this conflict confidential from everyone—in a way even from myself. As a way of coping, I never let people know I loved them or valued them. Doing so only empowered them and their ability to hurt me. I was locked in a painful cycle of embrace and retreat. Such strategies came with a cost.

Regarding my relationship with God, I settled on serving him with my hands instead of also loving him with my heart. Regarding my relationship with people, I only let people in so far.

I justified this approach because it was safer and cleaner. Preferring transactional relationships instead of transformational ones, I wouldn't let myself feel "weak" enough to need relationships. I deceived myself into thinking true strength meant independence. I craved an illusion, a life without pain— but the price of such a life is also one without love.

God had a strange way of leading me to give up the Name Game, a necessary precursor to discovering my Secret Name. Love knocked on my heart and, when I opened the door to let her in, pain followed close behind.

Jacob dispatched a peace offering to Esau. (Call it a backup plan just in case God didn't protect him.) Without the Internet or television, he didn't have much to do except wait.

And wonder.

What if Esau was still angry? What if Esau's four hundred men were coming to rape and kill him and his entourage? What if God forgot about his promise to bless and keep him—or what if God was unable to stop his brother? One thing was certain: sleep didn't visit Jacob that evening.

A temporary insomniac, Jacob ordered his entire camp to pack up and leave. He needed the illusion of controlling something in his chaotic life, and so he took his two wives, his two maidservants, and his eleven sons and made them do a march at midnight.

After he had sent them across the stream, he sent over all his possessions and his livestock. This was no easy task, especially in the middle of the night and over water. But when everyone crossed safely, the Scriptures tell us, "Jacob was left alone" on one side of the river. In his darkest hour, he was left alone to wrestle with his thoughts.

I started the first semester of graduate school apprehensively, knowing all too well the horror stories about the difficulty of the seminary's counseling track. My mentor, Dr. Plaster, who also served as the vice president, encouraged this track because, in his mind, it would better prepare me to be a military chaplain. I followed his recommendation, but at the moment all it seemed like twice the work.

Under the seminary banner, I had Greek and Hebrew classes to confound my brain, while under the counseling banner I had addictive disorders and abnormal psychology classes to challenge my soul.

Relatively early in the semester, while sitting in one of my counseling classes, I noticed a new girl. Our classes were so small it was easy to notice anybody new. But there was something different about her. I found myself drawn to her, without even thinking about it. This new girl—Kelly—often walked in extremely late and extremely confident. More than once I found myself tuning into her instead of the professor giving the lecture.

It was more than her appearance—though her soft brown hair and hazel eyes were much more interesting than my textbook. Rather, it was her responses to the class discussions that captivated me most. Fresh and alive, the words she used and the way she said them sounded like someone who was free. The more I listened and watched the clearer it became. Kelly seemed unrestrained and uninhibited—quite the opposite of me!

One day after class I asked a friend if I could borrow his book. Although he declined because he hadn't completed the assignment, Kelly offered hers.

So after class on that autumn day, with leaves changing to brilliant reds, yellows, and oranges, we walked back to her apartment so I could pick up the book. I was a bit surprised when she asked me if I wanted to come inside, but even more surprised when I followed her upstairs.

African masks hung on her walls. A beaded curtain posing as a makeshift wall separated the living room from the small kitchen. On another wall hung posters displaying a variety of musicians, art, and photography. We both liked many of the same less-than-common bands, and two and a half hours later, with a stack of her CDs in my hand, I invited her to visit my apartment down the street to borrow some of my music. To my surprise, she agreed.

I asked Kelly to wait outside on the stairs in order for me to "straighten up" my room. In reality, I wanted to brief my roommate Gary so he could give me his opinion. I told him to act normal, stay ten minutes, and then leave to "study" at the library. I asked him to call our apartment later and give me his opinion of her. I wanted his insight, but I already knew the answer.

Kelly and I spent another two and a half hours swapping music and more laughter. Gary called promptly with his approval, but by then I didn't care what he thought of her. In a five-hour period, Kelly sucker-punched my heart. I had no idea what the future held for us, if anything, but I felt more emotionally alive than I had in years.

Four days later, after class, she invited me to her apartment again. Feeling she was worth the risk, I told her I saw in her a freedom that left me stunned and wanting more. She came clean too, saying she could see herself spending the rest of her life with me. Right then and there, we officially began our relationship.

A month later I spent two hours trying to tell her why I would not kiss her. After I made my logic known, we spent a large part of that evening kissing. My emotional walls started tumbling down—brick-by-brick.

Four months later, I drove to Michigan to ask Kelly's dad if I could marry his daughter. A month after that, Kelly and I took a walk at sunset on the shore of Lake Michigan. We "stumbled" upon a bonfire and a gourmet picnic. I asked a couple of her friends to secretly capture the whole ordeal on film.

I wasn't expecting it to be an action movie—she started out by punching me for "pulling one over on her." But in the next scene, I dropped to one knee and produced a ring. Lucky me, she said yes.

We set our wedding date for six months later—October 14—a year to the day of our first meeting.

Life would have been great if it hadn't been for those wretched counseling classes. They were peeling back layers of my soul, and I didn't appreciate the fact the professors didn't use anesthesia. Layers of self-protective strategies, coping mechanisms, and stoicism crumbled before me. Being engaged to Kelly opened me up to a world of color and emotion.

Most of the time, I didn't know how I felt because feelings seemed so foreign to me. Instead of walking away, Kelly graciously took my hand and walked right beside me. She wouldn't let me slip away.

I told her about my first visit to a counselor at the age of ten. She encouraged me to contact my pediatrician's office for a release of medical forms, believing those notes from the past might shed some light on my present dilemma and offer me hope for the future—or more correctly put, hope for *our* future.

I often say it was cheaper to marry a counselor than to visit one. I followed Kelly's advice and requested my file.

The medical notes detailed my depressed mental state as

a child. My parents noticed "irritability, anger, ease of frustration, and concern about the death of his parents as well as discomfort with staying overnight with friends or relatives." Because of this, they brought their concerns to my pediatrician, who suggested a psychiatric consultation.

I remember two things from that appointment: #1, my dad helped me fill out the questionnaire, because at ten years old I didn't really know how, and #2, I lied about my answer to one of his questions.

He read from the form, "Have you ever attempted or thought of suicide?" Although in the session notes, the blank is checked "no" with my dad's handwriting, I remember at the time wanting to say yes. But how does a ten-year-old broach the topic of suicidal thoughts with his dad?

On the last page of enclosed documents, I saw a photocopied piece of notebook paper with a handwritten note. My mom had briefed the doctor, explaining why she was unable to attend the assessment:

Dear Dr. Todd,
 I really wish more than anything to be with Kary and Mike this afternoon for the appointment with you. Perhaps you'll let me share a few comments and observations:
 Changes in personality gradually occurring involving:

- *tearful daily*
- *outbursts of anger*
- *anxiousness*
- *homesickness*
- *fear of death of himself, Mike, and I*

Whatever illness I presently have has greatly helped Kary over the fear he had of being without me.
 Sincerely, Linda

This note stuffed into my chart produced the missing puzzle piece for the cause of my depression. No wonder I needed to go to a counselor. Mom wasn't at the appointment because she had had two unexplainable strokes. I distinctly remember visiting her in the hospital, desperately scared of losing her. Instead of processing my fears externally, I stuffed them internally, hence the tearfulness, anger, anxiety, homesickness, and fear of my parents dying.

My need for counseling as a ten-year-old centered on a depression that stemmed from my mother almost dying. Throughout my childhood, Mom had several other close calls. A few years earlier, she had a near-fatal ruptured appendix that required an invasive surgery and a year of recovery.

When I was sixteen, my father suffered a severe heart attack that nearly took his life. I underwent another season of depression, which climaxed with one of my first cutting episodes. I detested death, and the thought of my parents dying scared me to death. Cutting gave me the illusion of controlling pain instead of letting it control me.

In these seasons of crises, we didn't have time for family meetings where I could process my pain—at least I can't remember such meetings. But even if we did, I'm not so sure they would have helped. I felt like I had nowhere to go with my feelings. I couldn't go to God because I was furious with him. And even if I knew God could handle my anger, I would have felt guilty for even being angry at him in the first place. In my mind, anger toward God wasn't something allowed.

Besides, asking God for anything was out of the question. Such a strategy meant entering a relationship with him, and I most certainly didn't want that. Relationships were the source of my pain, and although I was willing to work for God with my hands, loving him with my heart was a thought I quickly pushed from my head.

So rather than wrestling with God, I chose isolation.

But like Jacob, all alone on my side of the river, God came to wrestle me instead.

13

THE DIVINE WOUND

Wrestling with your thoughts alone in the middle of the night can be scary. Just ask Jacob. Wrestling with *God* in the middle of the night is even scarier. Again, ask Jacob. Standing solo on his side of the river, Jacob was visited by a powerful being who engaged Jacob in a no-holds-barred wrestling match.

The author of Genesis describes Jacob's opponent as a "man." Many biblical scholars believe this mysterious man was none other than God himself, a phenomenon called a "theophany," a Greek word that describes the appearance of God to humans. The prophet Hosea confirms this, stating when Jacob "struggled with the angel" he actually "struggled with God."

Jacob didn't pick this fight, God did. On the eve of confronting Esau, an event in which Jacob's past, present, and future collided, God initiated a struggle.

Left to our own devices, we usually choose the path of least resistance and prefer stagnation over transformation. It's a good thing God doesn't give in to our preferences. Instead, he engages us in a painful yet powerful transformative experience. So who won the match?

THE DIVINE WOUND

The man saw that he could not overpower him, [so] he touched the socket of Jacob's hip so that his hip was wrenched as he wrestled with the man.

Genesis 32:25

Did Jacob beat God? No more than I beat my father as a five-year-old when I "pinned" him on the living room floor.

At any moment God could have ended the match, but he didn't. Although he clearly "owned" the match, he let Jacob stay in the fight, a familiar practice in the Scriptures.[1]

The pace of the match was for Jacob's sake, not God's.

As a five-year-old wrestling my father, I was outmatched in size, strength, and age. My dad didn't wrestle me to show off or build his own confidence. He wrestled me so we would have an experience together—to build up my confidence and teach me moves. At any moment he could have ended the match, but instead he let me wrestle him, believing the illusion that I might be able to beat him.

The experience paid off. As I continued to wrestle throughout my life, I was no longer intimidated by my opponents since I regularly wrestled my father, someone much bigger and stronger than my peers.

God wrestled Jacob, knowing full well it was Jacob who needed to be stretched. Wrestling God until daybreak gave Jacob the confidence he needed to face less powerful opponents like Esau.

Dawn approached and he'd face Esau soon enough—but not before first facing an even darker moment.

During graduate school, I wished I could have been left alone with my thoughts. Unfortunately, like every other student, I had required meetings with my intern supervisor and my faculty adviser. Through videotaping and discussion, our counseling skills (or lack of skills) were reviewed, then scrutinized. The faculty believed that no matter how hard we studied, we couldn't develop our counseling skills unless we were willing to interface with real people and real problems.

We were taught that we could help other people work through their pain only if we had first worked through our own pain, and good counselors were the type of people who, although imperfect, were courageous in facing their own issues.

I tried to be one of these courageous people. In my weekly sessions with my supervisor, I let my guard down. I wanted to look honestly at the fears and inadequacies that had their hooks in my heart.

My supervisor and adviser did their best to help me process my thoughts and emotions. For years I had stuffed my feelings and withdrawn from certain relational dynamics, like expressing affection and appreciation. Consequently, I found it exceptionally difficult to understand and discuss my clients' pain.

Each time I received a negative evaluation—I needed to be more empathetic, I needed to engage with my clients more, I needed to allow them to express pain without trying to fix them—I accepted the assessment and attempted to improve both myself and my counseling. It was agonizing.

Although I felt compassion for my clients, I feared that getting too close to their pain would increase my pain as well. Running from my own identity issues, how could I encourage them to face theirs?

The semester got the best of me. My faculty adviser gave me poor marks at my midterm evaluation. Although I aced the materials academically, in his opinion I was failing the class emotionally.

My intern supervisor didn't feel any different. She commented I might not pass the class and encouraged me to rethink my enrollment in the counseling program. Their comments ripped into me. *I was trying my best. Couldn't they see that?*

THE DIVINE WOUND

Like I had feared, entering this new world of feelings and emotions had chewed me up and spit me out. I was angry. I felt betrayed and misunderstood. As soon as I had begun to fly, my wings were clipped, and I came crashing down. Words couldn't communicate my rage, and I chose a knife as a means of expression, punishing myself for feeling. Without a developed outlet for emotional expression, I chose the only relief I knew—cutting.

Although my supervisor was the source of my relational pain only minutes before, in the privacy of my apartment I was the one who controlled the physical pain. I held the blade. This transfer of power put me back in control.

In the safety of my room, no one could hurt me but me. I looked down at my wounds, blood now pooling on my forearms and upper thighs. Carved in scarlet, I gave myself several names. Beside cuss words, I wrote: FAILURE, EMPTY, ALONE.

Although I was numb, my physical pain quickly reverted to emotional pain. I couldn't escape the deep hole in my heart, and I wanted to give up on this new world of feelings.

I went to the bathroom and pulled toilet paper from the roll. The white sheets turned bright red as I wiped them across the fresh wounds on my arms. With mechanical movements, I continued to clean myself, tossing the paper into the toilet. The red water in the bowl was my only witness. With one simple flush, I'd protect my charade one more time and continue pretending.

But this time something different happened.

My eye caught the bathroom mirror and I saw a face staring back at me—one I didn't even recognize. I looked deep into the glass, deeper than I had in years.

I saw a face full of anguish and pain—eyes heavy and tired. Who was this person? What had I become? Who was I becoming?

The strangeness of seeing myself as a stranger stopped me.

Here I was, a boy covered in blood, running from my past and, in the process, destroying my future. I couldn't take any more. My dissatisfaction was too strong. And my longing for a new name was too powerful. I couldn't live another day as an imposter in my own skin.

In that moment, I awoke.

My Given Name was silenced, and for the first time, I was ready to receive my Secret Name.

Jacob kept fighting.

His Secret Name had eluded him for far too long. The years back home, the lonely nights in exile, and the long days working for Laban all collided into one single moment—a wrestling match with God Almighty.

God wanted to transform Jacob, but transformation is never easy, and it always involves pain. Thankfully, on the other side of pain is promise—the promise of our Secret Name. God initiates a divine wound in order to help us shed our old skin and step fully into our new identity. Author Oswald Chambers said it best. "Before God can use a man greatly, he must wound him deeply."[2]

Even though at times it hurts like hell—literally—we simply *must* stay in the fight.

God never promised we wouldn't have pain. He only promised he'd walk through it with us.[3] Like Jacob, our limp may last a lifetime, but our Secret Name lasts forever.

In this final stage, many of us give up and go back home to our Given Names. Wrestling God takes its toll, and even though we're only inches away from a new identity, we let it slip away once more.

Jacob stuck it out.

Jacob was left alone, and a man wrestled with him till daybreak. When the man saw that he could not overpower him, he touched the socket of Jacob's hip so that his hip was wrenched as he wrestled with the man.

Genesis 32:24–25

Jacob pushed through the pain, adamant and resolute he'd receive a blessing or die trying. He embodied a quality called "importunity"—a trait most people know nothing about. Importunity means that we incessantly and compulsively make our request known.[4] With a fierce resolve, we won't quit until our desire is fulfilled. Jacob embodied the very essence of importunity, resolved not to give up.

Then the man said, "Let me go, for it is daybreak." But Jacob replied, "I will not let you go unless you bless me."

Genesis 32:26

God wanted to leave—or at least he gave that impression. and this impression inspired Jacob, emboldening him to ask for a blessing. Little did Jacob know, with that very gesture, he was actually embodying his Secret Name, which in a matter of moments would no longer be a secret.

Sensing his strong commitment, the angel asked, "What is your name?"

Interesting how Jacob asked for a blessing and the angel responded by asking him his name. Perhaps within that exchange, we stumble upon a secret. Seems like many of us crave a blessing—we want God to bless us, our families, our jobs, and our finances. Thank God that he doesn't just snap his fingers and grant us our wish.

Instead, God knows our only shot at a true blessing comes by uncovering our true identity. But before we can discover our Secret Name, we must first confess our Given Name—a pattern found throughout the Bible.

Jesus illustrated this principle in one of his interactions. In the gospel of Mark, Jesus encountered a man tormented by demons. This man—a cutter—suffered from issues related to his misplaced identity.

> *This man lived in the tombs, and no one could bind him any more, not even with a chain. For he had often been chained hand and foot, but he tore the chains apart and broke the irons on his feet. No one was strong enough to subdue him. Night and day among the tombs and in the hills he would cry out and cut himself with stones.*
>
> Mark 5:3–5

This demon-possessed man held some fairly inaccurate views of God, believing that God was out to harm him:

> *When he saw Jesus from a distance, he ran and fell on his knees in front of him. He shouted at the top of his voice, "What do you want with me, Jesus, Son of the Most High God? Swear to God that you won't torture me!" For Jesus had said to him, "Come out of this man, you evil spirit!"*
>
> Mark 5:6–8

Jesus, the Son of God, utilized an interesting strategy that was critical in this man's healing process. Jesus asked him a penetrating question: "What is your name?" Of course, he already knew the man's name—he's God, after all. The question wasn't for his sake, but rather for the man's. Jesus wanted the man to verbalize his inaccurate identity.

The man replied, "My name is Legion…for we are many." By the man confessing his Given Name, Jesus was then able to endow him with a Secret Name. This was the rationale behind Jesus' question, and it's also the rationale behind the angel's question to Jacob.

God didn't ask Jacob his name because he didn't know it. God asked Jacob his name in order to see if he'd admit it.

Ouch—and Jacob thought the dislocated hip hurt!

The last time Jacob was asked his name, the circumstances were a bit different. He stood before his earthly father, Isaac, as an imposter—wearing someone else's identity. He said his name was Esau and, by lying, Jacob embodied the very essence of his Given Name—DECEIVER. He played that part perfectly.

Now he was locked in a wrestling match with his heavenly Father.

Would he lie again?

This time things were different. Finished with living as an imposter, Jacob decided to quit lying to himself and take off the mask. Charades got him nowhere, except stuck.

By answering the question honestly—"Jacob"—he gave up his Given Name. Although he couldn't have deceived God no matter what name he gave, Jacob had spent a lifetime deceiving himself. No longer content with pretending, his honest answer revealed the truth—that he was finally ready to receive his Secret Name.

I knew what I had to do.

I walked into the office of my intern supervisor, ready to finally renounce my Given Name. I was ready to end my pretending, my masquerading, and my isolation. I wasn't free yet—I still needed to hear my Secret Name, uttered from the lips of my Father. But, like Jacob, I stood ready to embody my new name. My time for hiding was over.

I sat down, looked at my supervisor, and rolled up my sleeves.

14

THE WHITE STONE

By owning up to his past name, Jacob proved he was finally ready to embrace his future one.

> *Then the man said, "Your name will no longer be Jacob, but Israel, because you have struggled with God and with men and have overcome."*
>
> Genesis 32:28

Those words fell as new white snow falls on the tired cold ground in the dead of winter. The landscape suddenly felt a little brighter.

No longer named Jacob—but now *Israel*.

Israel had a nice ring to it, but more than that, it contained deep symbolic overtones. *Israel* had both present implications—"one who strives with God," and future implications—"he will be a prince with God."

The new name reflected the reality that Jacob shifted from a weak position, known for scheming and deceiving, to a strong one, known for struggling and prevailing. Rather than stepping away from conflict through manipulation and dishonest tactics, he learned to step toward conflict through boldness and importunity. His transformation resulted from the divine wound—a dislocated hip—which he'd remember the rest of his life. Jacob and those who knew him would never be the same.

Secret Names aren't simply granted. They're also meant to be embodied. Jacob did just that. He wrapped his Secret Name around his shoulders and walked forward into his new identity.

By coming clean, I proved I was ready to receive my new name. Confessing to my intern supervisor took courage, and I danced close to freedom, but I had yet to hear my Secret Name.

Several days after my confession, while cleaning my bedroom, I stumbled across a novel my mother had given me titled *A White Stone*, written by my friend Jim Corbett, the disc jockey from Wisconsin who gave me that $500 for college. The title is taken from an obscure verse buried in Revelation.

> *He who has an ear, let him hear what the Spirit says to the churches. To him who overcomes, I will give some of the hidden manna. I will also give him a white stone with a new name written on it, known only to him who receives it.*
>
> Revelation 2:17

Secret Names written on white stones? Sounds like fiction, except it's not. This little-known verse carries tremendous implications, both in this life and the next.

Notice the recipient of the white stone—to him who *overcomes*. Sound familiar? Secret Names are reserved for only those who overcome—like Jacob being renamed Israel, meaning one who struggles with God and man and *overcomes*. The connection between this passage in Genesis and the one in Revelation is startling and comforting all at once. Turns out Secret Names are a theme throughout the entire Bible.

On the surface, white stones might not mean much to us in the twenty-first century, but they were incredibly significant to the first-century audience. White stones have everything to do with people from every generation in search of their true identities.

In antiquity, a time and place of multiculturalism, white stones served two important purposes—one dealing with innocence and the other with admittance.

In the court of justice, the color of a stone communicated a person's destiny. Jurors cast a white or dark stone—the white one symbolizing acquittal and acceptance. The dark meaning condemnation, blame, and rejection.

This understanding of the dark stone seeps into our current culture as seen in the term "blackball." The word *blackball* means to "ostracize" or "boycott," "to vote against…by casting a negative vote…to exclude socially."[1]

Back to antiquity: The Greek word for stone in Revelation 2:27—*psephos*—is found in only one other place in the New Testament, Acts 26:10, which refers to this judicial custom. Nearly two thousand years ago, prior to his conversion, the apostle Paul condemned many Christians to death according to his own confession:

> *And that is just what I did in Jerusalem. On the authority of the chief priests I put many of the saints in prison, and when they were put to death, I cast my vote [psephos] against them.*
> Acts 26:10

Although Paul was guilty of murder, he found a new life and a new name through Jesus Christ. As a forgiven man he wrote, "Therefore, if anyone is in Christ, he is a new creation; the old has gone, the new has come!"

God writes our Secret Name on a white stone, indicating our innocence. That same white stone is literally granted to us upon our entrance into heaven and serves as our invitation to feast with God forever.

THE WHITE STONE

In the first century, because they didn't have printing presses to make tickets, admittance to prestigious events or banquets was granted by issuing a white stone with one's name on it. Guests would present their white stones to the attendant at the gate prior to entering the respective banquet.

Those of us whose new names are written on white stones will join every other child of God throughout history at a breathtaking banquet with the eternal Trinity.

Holding Jim's book in my hand on that spring afternoon, my mind raced back to the last time I saw him, four years ago, before I left for Indiana. Everything suddenly stopped for a split second—both my breathing and my thoughts. Jim's curious smile and charismatic demeanor came rushing back into my mind—his parting words still a fresh deposit in my memory bank, "I think the Father wants you to have this."

GALATIANS 5:1—that forgotten verse! I hadn't thought about it in four years, much less looked up the reference.

I grabbed my Bible and leafed through the pages at a panicked pace. Somehow I knew I would hear from my God. My eyes confirmed what my soul already knew—I was about to receive my Secret Name.

> *It is for freedom that Christ has set us free. Stand firm, then, and do not let yourselves be burdened again by a yoke of slavery.*
> Galatians 5:1

These words leaped off the page, capturing the incredible angst that had consumed me the last twenty-three years of my life. Although I probably read that verse before, I never *heard* it. Perhaps it had flown over my head in a lecture, but on this ordinary afternoon, it hit me in a new way.

But then something else happened—even stranger yet. One of those twenty-six words spoke to me in a way I'd never quite experienced before.

The word FREE.
FREE.
This is your Secret Name.
I've wanted to give it to you for a long time, but you weren't ready.
Up until now, you were just content pretending.
FREE.
This is who you were born to be.
This is your true identity.
This is who you are.
FREE.

My Secret Name wasn't a destination, and learning it didn't mean life was ending. As I soon found out, discovering my Secret Name meant that life was just about to begin.

Walking in my new name wasn't easy. I quickly learned I'd always have a limp. My journey eventually led me to a total of three different counselors and countless journal entries. God lovingly brought trial after trial into my life, which made me confront my new name. After all, what's the point of a Secret Name if you never wear it?

My first test came when I received my spring semester grades. To my shock, my faculty adviser failed me, evidently believing my issues disqualified me from being an effective counselor. In the comment section of my report, he seriously questioned my ability to help others when I was so in need of help myself.

This time, however, I had a new name—*FREE*—and I strengthened myself in that truth rather than in his lie. My faculty adviser no longer had the power to name me a failure. And indeed, my mentor, Dr. Plaster, soon stepped in and overruled his decision, allowing me to pass the class, aware of my sincere efforts to experience healing and pass that healing on to others.

Through a series of circumstances, the real truth surfaced—my faculty adviser, in a marriage himself, had been having an affair with a married student in our program. Perhaps his own conscience was tormented by his recent choices, and he chose me as an easy target to pass off his personal pain.

A few months after graduating, I saw my former adviser in the locker room at the YMCA. Although my Given Name urged me to ignore him or perhaps even relish in his defeat—his professorship recently stripped from him— my Secret Name spoke to him a kind hello, genuinely grieving for his self-inflicted wounds.

Step after painful step, I strengthened my Secret Name.

As the morning sun rose above the river, Jacob had a choice to flee or to face his brother. He had hidden behind his Given Name his entire life, and unfortunately, Esau didn't know Jacob's new name, Israel. The only way Esau could realize Jacob's new name would be to see it standing before him.

Jacob knew he had to walk in his new name and so, rather than running away, he extended a kind hello.

> *[Jacob] went on ahead and bowed down to the ground seven times as he approached his brother. But Esau ran to meet Jacob and embraced him; he threw his arms around his neck and kissed him. And they wept.*
>
> Genesis 33:3–4

Evidently over his anger, Esau forgave his brother and invited Jacob to join him on his journey. Jacob knew he couldn't go with Esau. He had a new identity, and with that new name he also had a new calling.

When we receive our Secret Name, we can't continue with life as normal. By embracing our new identity, we also embrace our new destiny and a new way of seeing the world.

The two go hand in hand. Because we live in dynamic relationships and not static ones, when our name changes, so do our relationships.

Esau's path took him to Seir, Jacob's to Succoth.

End of story, right?

Hardly.

No more than my story ending with a diploma on graduation day. Receiving your Secret Name isn't the end of the story. It's only the start.

15
SACRED SPACES

You might be wondering, "How's that new name working for you?"

Fair question—I'd want to know.

Here's the truth. My Secret Name works for me only when I work for it. Every morning I have the option of strapping on my Given Names or walking in my new name.[1]

The difference is that at least now I know. Prior to discovering my Secret Name, I operated as a lost boy in search of who he truly was. Now I know who I am, but I still have a choice to live in the light of it. Every talk I give, every relationship I have, every confrontation I face, and every day I live, I have the opportunity to exist according to my Secret Name—FREE—or my previous Given Names—STUTTERER, CUTTER, FAILURE, ENSLAVED.

Although I never want to forget my Secret Name, I also never want to forget my Given Names either. They're who *I was*, not who *I am*. Besides, remembering my brokenness helps me stay compassionate toward others still in their brokenness.

When referencing Jacob, the human writers of the Bible utilize a similar flip-flop pattern found hundreds of places throughout the pages of Scripture. They frequently go back and forth, referring to Jacob as "Jacob" long after he had been renamed Israel.

YOUR SECRET NAME

The Bible uses "Jacob"—his Given Name—339 times. But Jacob's Secret Name, "Israel," is used much more—1,695 times to be exact. So why the constant flip-flopping?

Although God endows us with a Secret Name, he never wants us to forget our Given Names. Remembering them—not living by them, but just remembering them—produces humility and gratitude. Humility, because we know our Secret Name is more about God than us. Gratitude, because we know what we've been saved from.

The person who does the saving, of course, is Jesus—at least that's his Given Name. But as I found out, even the Son of God has a Secret Name.

> *His eyes are like blazing fire, and on his head are many crowns. He has a name written on him that no one knows but he himself.*
>
> Revelation 19:12

Wouldn't we all like to know the identity of this mysterious person? The context makes it clear that this rider mounted on a white horse is Jesus himself. But the context also makes it clear that Jesus isn't his real name. Like us, the Son of God also has a Secret Name. Amazingly, other passages support this mystery, even the ones that seem to contradict it on the surface. Check out Philippians:

> *And being found in appearance as a man, he humbled himself and became obedient to death—even death on a cross! Therefore God exalted him to the highest place and gave him the name that is above every name, that at the name of Jesus every knee should bow, in heaven and on earth and under the earth, and every tongue confess that Jesus Christ is Lord, to the glory of God the Father.*
>
> Philippians 2:8–11

Jesus is a great name, but thousands of people have had that name both now and in the past. So why is the name Jesus above every other name?

The truth is, it's not.

The more we study this passage, the more we see that "Jesus" isn't the superior name referenced in Philippians. Rather, Jesus received an additional name—a Secret Name—so powerful that all of creation will hit the floor upon hearing it.

A closer look reveals three reasons why Jesus isn't the superior name and why he must have a Secret Name too.

1. The Exclusivity of the name.
In the original Greek, the apostle Paul uses the definite article before the word *name*. He's telling us that there is one name superior to every other name. It is *THE* name, meaning that Jesus alone has it. Hebrews 1:4 supports this claim, stating: "He became as much superior to the angels as the name he has inherited is superior to theirs." This verse makes it clear that Jesus' name is superior to every human name and to every angelic name as well.

2. The Rationale for the name.
Jesus received his superior name because of what he did—specifically that he "humbled himself and became obedient to death—even death on a cross." The new name emerges because of his obedience, not simply his birth. Paul makes this clear by using the word *therefore* in verse 9, signifying why Jesus received this name—as a result of embracing his unique destiny.

3. The Timing of the name.
An angel told Joseph to bestow the name of Jesus upon the new child at the time of his grand entrance on earth. "You are to give him the name Jesus, because he will save his people

from their sins." In Philippians, Paul told us that God alone (not Joseph) granted Jesus the superior name and that the timing of this endowment occurred at his exaltation after his death, not at his birth.

The exclusivity, rationale, and timing of this superior name make it clear that the name Jesus doesn't make the cut. Rather, Jesus' Secret Name came from the lips of his heavenly Father upon completion of his assignment here on earth.

Although divine, Jesus laid aside such privileges in order to enter our world. He didn't hover around as some quasi-human spirit, immune from the brokenness here on earth. Rather, he stepped into our story, including the dynamics of dealing with a Given Name.

He heard the jokes—the ones about the little bastard child born in Bethlehem. Rumors undoubtedly circled about Mary's "supposed virgin birth." Jesus suffered through life as an insignificant, impoverished man, without worldly power, or stunning appearance. He embraced that life, and the Given Name Jesus, realizing that in the end he'd receive his Secret Name—the "name above every other name."

> *During the days of Jesus' life on earth, he offered up prayers and petitions with loud cries and tears to the one who could save him from death, and he was heard because of his reverent submission. Although he was a son, he learned obedience from what he suffered and, once made perfect, he became the source of eternal salvation for all who obey him.*
> Hebrews 5:7–9

The story of Jesus is simple. As a result of strapping on human skin, Jesus naturally strapped on Given Names as well. By walking in this world, he tasted the pain that plagues us all. And even though it hurt like hell, Jesus still went there to set us free. He took on a Given Name and exchanged his own life that we might discover our Secret Name.

When we do discover our own Secret Name, something odd takes place. In that moment we end up discovering God's Secret Names. Moses happened to be one of the first people to experience this unique phenomenon, but he certainly wasn't the last.

Remember Moses? He spent forty years enjoying the riches of Egypt in the palace feasting on his Given Name—ADOPTED SON OF PHARAOH. With a fortune at his fingertips, Moses knew something even bigger lay in the cards for him.

His Given Names got the best of him, and he forced his destiny a little too fast. After burying the evidence—one dead Egyptian slave master—he fled for his life, just happy to get out of town alive. Exiled into the desert with a forty-year sentence, he inherited one more Given Name—SHEPHERD. His life eventually achieved equilibrium—until that infamous bush caught fire and started speaking to him. God knew he needed to use something drastic to wake up this former prince of Egypt, now turned caretaker of sheep.

Through this eventful exchange, God gave Moses a glimpse of his Secret Name—DELIVERER. At that moment, unknown to himself, Moses responded with a very normal question, "Who am I?" Unfazed, God weighed in with an answer that seemed to avoid the question just a little, "I will be with you."

Like most humans on a new quest with God, Moses then shot back another normal question, "What is [your] name?" God's answer revealed that by getting a snapshot of our own Secret Name, we inevitably find one of his Secret Names too.

God said to Moses, "I am who I am. This is what you are to say to the Israelites: 'I Am has sent me to you.'" God also said to Moses, "Say to the Israelites, 'The Lord, the God of your fathers—the God of Abraham, the God of Isaac and the God of Jacob—has sent me to you.' This is my name forever, the name by which I am to be remembered from generation to generation.

Exodus 3:14–15

Although we usually start with ourselves as the center, we eventually come to understand that God is the ultimate focus. The pattern holds true. As we discover who *we* truly are, we also discover a portion of who *he* truly is.

Peeling back the layers of God's reply to Moses' question ("What is your name?") reveals a rich pattern related to God's Secret Names. "I am who I am," literally means "He will be to them what His deeds show Him to be." Breaking it down, God tells Moses that his name will be whatever his attributes reveal him to be. For example, when God protects a certain individual, then to that person God is known by the name PROTECTOR.

As strange as it sounds, the more we experience God, the more of his Secret Names we experience. Consider just a few of God's names from the Bible:

ELOHIM = "God" (plural) as in the Creator.
  Genesis 1:1
EL ELYON = "God (singular) Most High." Genesis 14:18–20
EL ROI = "God Who Sees." Genesis 16:13–14
EL SHADDAI = "God Almighty." Genesis 17:1
EL OLAM = "The Everlasting God." Genesis 21:33
JEHOVAH JIREH = "The Lord Will Provide."
  Genesis 22:14
ADONAI = "Lord." Exodus 4:10–11
YAHWEH = "Personal name for God." Exodus 4:10
JEHOVAH-RAPHA = "The Lord who heals."
  Exodus 15:26

JEHOVAH-NISSI = "The Lord is my Banner." Exodus 17:15

QANNA = "Jealous." Exodus 20:5

JEHOVAH-MEKADDISHKEM = "The Lord Who Sanctifies You." Exodus 31:13

JEHOVAH-SHALOM = "The Lord is Peace." Judges 6:22–24

JEHOVAH-SABAOTH = "The Lord of Hosts." Psalm 22:10

JEHOVAH-ROHI = "The Lord is my Shepherd." Psalm 23:1

JEHOVAH-TSIDKENU = "The Lord Our Righteousness." Jeremiah 23:5–6

JEHOVAH-SHAMMAH = "the Lord is there." Ezekiel 48:35

God's names are numerous, tucked away in every book of the Bible. I found one list with over 700 names for Jesus alone. Add God the Father and the Spirit and this list tops well over a thousand different names.

Surprised? I'm not.

Why wouldn't the Creator of life possess endless attributes expressed by countless names?

What *does* surprise me is that God permits and even takes pleasure in us naming him—the creation names the Creator. The Bible often shows God's people naming his unique attributes after *experiencing* his unique attributes.

Hagar, the mother of Ishmael, upon realizing that God understood her unique situation, gave God the name EL ROI. "She gave this name to the Lord who spoke to her: 'You are the God who sees me,' for she said, 'I have now seen the One who sees me.'"

Abraham, the father of the nation of Israel, upon finding the ram that God provided, gave God the name JEHOVAH JIREH, The Lord Will Provide.

Moses, the deliverer of Israel, upon experiencing victory over the Amalekites, gave God the name JEHOVAH-NISSI, The Lord is my Banner.

David, the king of Israel, upon experiencing safety through the valley of the shadow of death, gave God the name JEHOVAH-ROHI, the Lord is my Shepherd.

I, upon experiencing freedom from my Given Name, gave God the name EL DEROR, the God who liberates.

My Secret Name for God reflects the specific way in which I experienced God's healing. With ENSLAVED as my Given Name and FREE as my Secret Name, EL DEROR—the God who Liberates—makes sense. EL DEROR reflects the ultimate reason why the Son of God came to earth.

> "The Spirit of the Lord is on me, because he has anointed me to preach good news to the poor. He has sent me to proclaim freedom for the prisoners and recovery of sight for the blind, to release the oppressed, to proclaim the year of the Lord's favor."
>
> Luke 4:18–19

Jacob practiced this pattern of naming God as well. When Jacob discovered his Secret Name (Israel), he immediately tried to discover God's Secret Name.

> The man asked him, "What is your name?"
> "Jacob," he answered.
> Then the man said, "Your name will no longer be Jacob, but Israel, because you have struggled with God and with men and have overcome."
> Jacob said, "Please tell me your name."
>
> Genesis 32:27–29

Regardless of Jacob's question, he didn't actually need to *learn* God's Secret Name. He already *knew* it because he had already experienced it. Asking to physically hear it only produced a puzzled reply.

> *But he replied, "Why do you ask my name?"*
> Genesis 32:29

God's reply forced Jacob to reflect on what he knew to be true. Jacob had already discovered God's Secret Name, and so he spoke it aloud: "PENIEL," meaning "I saw God face to face." Jacob memorialized his experience with God by permanently attaching this new name to that exact location—a Sacred Space for centuries to come.

To this day my parents still live near the same place where they grew up. When we were young, an interesting event occurred repeatedly. The family would be traveling in the minivan when suddenly my dad would make a quick turn and launch into a story about their first house just up the road on the left.

My mom would jump in with details about the color of the walls and the name of their dog, their combined recollections translated into a time warp right before our eyes.

We kids were immediately whisked out of our little worlds, richer knowing we were part of a larger story. Seeing our parents excited—now sitting closer together in the minivan and smiling at each other—made us feel even more secure. Without intending to, we were guilty of tiptoeing on a Sacred Space.

We all have them—Sacred Spaces.

One of mine is Lake Michigan—the place I went after I received Carl's message that God couldn't afford to have me discouraged because he was going to use me in a significant way.

Growing up in Milwaukee, I often enjoyed the west side of Lake Michigan— spending large amounts of time reading my Bible, praying, journaling, and dreaming about what life might bring. I first met God on those sandy shores—offering him the only thing I knew: my future.

The search for my Secret Name took me to a variety of other places, but a few years later I returned to my roots and proposed to Kelly on the shore of Lake Michigan. Born only eighty miles away from Milwaukee, Wisconsin, Kelly grew up in Michigan looking at the same lake from a different vantage point—the east side.

Every Christmas season, Kelly and I return together to our hometowns to spend the holidays with our families. On New Year's Day, I slip away for a few hours to engage in a deeply meaningful tradition. Regardless of the weather, I head out to Lake Michigan with my Bible and my journal in order to take a hike through the woods. On a particular sand dune overlooking a winter landscape, I sit and review my journal entries from the previous year. It helps me stay grounded.

After reading, writing, questioning, and praying, I grab a handful of sand, representing of the number of minutes in my upcoming year. I this time to God, asking him to lead and direct me.

Then I throw that same handful into the air, symbolically offering it back to God. The puff of sand flies freely into the air and then, after a moment, it disappears—just like our lives.

Jacob's Sacred Space was Bethel, the location where God met him while in exile, on the run from his brother Esau. Remember the place?

> *When he reached a certain place, he stopped for the night because the sun had set. Taking one of the stones there, he put it under his head and lay down to sleep. He had a dream in which he saw a stairway resting on the earth, with its top reaching to heaven, and the angels of God were ascending and descending on it. There above it stood the Lord, and he*

said: "I am the Lord, the God of your father Abraham and the God of Isaac. I will give you and your descendants the land on which you are lying. Your descendants will be like the dust of the earth, and you will spread out to the west and to the east, to the north and to the south. All peoples on earth will be blessed through you and your offspring.

Genesis 28:11–14

Remember the promise?

"I am with you and will watch over you wherever you go, and I will bring you back to this land. I will not leave you until I have done what I have promised you." When Jacob awoke from his sleep, he thought, "Surely the Lord is in this place, and I was not aware of it." He was afraid and said, "How awesome is this place! This is none other than the house of God; this is the gate of heaven." Early the next morning Jacob took the stone he had placed under his head and set it up as a pillar and poured oil on top of it. He called that place Bethel, though the city used to be called Luz.

Genesis 28:15–19

Jacob first met God in that lonely location—offering him the only thing he knew, his future. On the search for his Secret Name, his quest led him to several other places, but many years later God brought him back to Bethel just as he promised. Jacob returned to the same Sacred Space, but now with a different vantage point and a new name.

Then God said to Jacob, "Go up to Bethel and settle there, and build an altar there to God, who appeared to you when you were fleeing from your brother Esau." So Jacob said to his household and to all who were with him, "Get rid of the foreign gods you have with you, and purify yourselves and change your clothes. Then come, let us go up to Bethel, where I will build an altar to God, who answered me in the day of my distress and who has been with me wherever I have gone."

So they gave Jacob all the foreign gods they had and the rings in their ears, and Jacob buried them under the oak at Shechem. Then they set out, and the terror of God fell upon the towns all around them so that no one pursued them. Jacob and all the people with him came to Luz (that is, Bethel) in the land of Canaan. There he built an altar, and he called the place El Bethel, because it was there that God revealed himself to him when he was fleeing from his brother.

Genesis 35:1–7

I don't pretend to know where you are right now in your quest to discover your Secret Name. You might be just starting or you might be well on your way. The important thing is that God knows. Nor do I pretend to know where you are in time and space. Again, God knows this too. He knows where you're sitting right now, and that place—your living room, a coffee shop, a park bench—can become a Sacred Space too.

God wants to meet you in your Sacred Space, and he's ready to make good on his promise.

"For I know the plans I have for you," declares the Lord, "plans to prosper you and not to harm you, plans to give you hope and a future. Then you will call upon me and come and pray to me, and I will listen to you. You will seek me and find me when you seek me with all your heart. I will be found by you," declares the Lord, "and will bring you back from captivity. I will gather you from all the nations and places where I have banished you," declares the Lord, "and will bring you back to the place from which I carried you into exile."

Jeremiah 29:11–14

Now is the time for you to awaken.

Now is the time for you to hear the Father whisper your Secret Name.

Now is the time for you to wrap your new identity around your shoulders and walk into the future God has prepared for you.

You hold in your hand a smooth white stone.

Your new name is written on it.

Welcome to the banquet.

We've been waiting for you.

Epilogue
First and Lasts

I try to pay attention to firsts in life: my first car, my first job, the first time my wife and I kissed.

Lasts are important too: my last wrestling match, my last college exam, the last time I said goodbye to my grandparents.

Beginnings and Endings are important in the Bible too. We open to page one and read, "In the beginning God," and then, many pages later, we read the last words of Jesus, "I am with you always."

The first time the Bible mentions the word *name* is Genesis 2:11. The author uses the Hebrew word *shem* when describing the rivers in Eden, "The *name* of the first is the Pishon; it winds through the entire land of Havilah, where there is gold."

If you're familiar with the story, you know that the garden of Eden is the heavenly paradise on earth, a Sacred Space rich with succulent food and breathtaking scenery. Hosting the Tree of Life, Eden was intended to be a place of profound relationship for God and his people, but we exchanged this glory by surrendering our Secret Names. We were expelled from Eden because we believed the lie that God was against us. Instead, we appropriated our Given Names, delivered by the Devil himself.

By forgetting God, we forgot who we were created to be.

But thankfully, this isn't the end of the story.

The last time the Bible mentions the word *name* is in Revelation 22:1–5, where the author uses the Greek word *onoma* when describing the citizens in heaven:

> *Then the angel showed me the river of the water of life, as clear as crystal, flowing from the throne of God and of the Lamb down the middle of the great street of the city. On each side of the river stood the tree of life, bearing twelve crops of fruit, yielding its fruit every month. And the leaves of the tree are for the healing of the nations. No longer will there be any curse. The throne of God and of the Lamb will be in the city, and his servants will serve him. They will see his face, and his name will be on their foreheads. There will be no more night. They will not need the light of a lamp or the light of the sun, for the Lord God will give them light. And they will reign forever and ever.*
>
> Revelation 22:1–5

The city of God—a place where every tear will cease and people from every nation will dwell in peace—will be inhabited by those of us who have embraced God's Secret Name. We'll wear it forever on our foreheads because we believe the truth that God is for us and created us to be his beloved children.

> *"It is done. I am the Alpha and the Omega, the Beginning and the End. To the thirsty I will give water without cost from the spring of the water of life. Those who are victorious will inherit all this, and I will be their God and they will be my children."*
>
> Revelation 21:6–7 TNIV

Let us come to the feast with great rejoicing, forever wearing our Secret Names, having discovered who we truly are—the people of God.

Appendix 1
Additional Insight on Secret Names

The Scriptures reveal several other privileged people who also received their Secret Name this side of eternity:

- *Abram*'s name, meaning "exalted father," was changed to *Abraham*, meaning "father of many nations."
- *Sarai*'s name, meaning "princess," was changed to *Sarah*, meaning "mother of many nations."
- Hosea's daughter's name *Lo-Ruhamah*, meaning "not loved," was changed to *Ruhamah*, meaning "loved."
- Hosea's son's name *Lo-Ammi*, meaning "not my -people," was changed to *Ammi*, meaning "my people."
- *Simon*'s name, meaning "obedient," was changed to *Peter*, meaning "rock."
- *Saul*'s name, meaning "desired" or "asked of God," was changed to *Paul*, meaning "little."

In each of these examples, the respective Secret Name revealed a distinctive destiny.

God invited these individuals into a transformational relationship whereby their Given Names would be relinquished in favor of a new, divinely led destiny. In each case, the path was as unique as the person.

Some individuals, like Simon and Saul, received their Secret Names immediately, relatively early in their quest. Others, like Abram and Sarai, received their Secret Names well into their expedition. Little is known about some individuals, like Ruhamah and Ammi, while much is known about others, like Peter and Paul.

Some people, like Abraham, Sarah, and Paul, were never again referred to by their Given Names. Others, like Simon/Peter, seemed to perpetually flip-flop between their Given Names and their Secret Names.

How did Jesus refer to this lead apostle? Remember, Jesus granted Simon with his new name Peter upon meeting him for the first time.

> *"Jesus looked at him and said, 'You are Simon son of John. You will be called Cephas' (which, when translated, is Peter)."*
> John 1:41–42

We tend to gloss over the oddity of this event. Next time you're introduced to the friend of a friend, perhaps at a party or a wedding reception, imagine if the person said, "I know your Birth Name, but from now on you will be called 'The Rock.'"

A little weird, to say the least.

Weirder still is the way Jesus refers to Peter throughout their three-year friendship—at times calling him by Simon, his Birth Name, and at other times by his new name, Peter. Sometimes, Jesus mixes it up—calling him both names from one sentence to the next. We see different nuances when reading different gospel writers and their record of Jesus' interactions with Peter.

ADDITIONAL INSIGHT ON SECRET NAMES

One possible explanation is that when this apostle seems to be steered by faith, embodying his new self, he's called Peter, and when he seems to be steered by fear, embodying his old self, he's called Simon. Notice a few examples:

"But what about you?" he asked. "Who do you say I am?"

Simon Peter answered, "You are the Christ, the Son of the living God."

Jesus replied, "Blessed are you, Simon son of Jonah, for this was not revealed to you by man, but by my Father in heaven. And I tell you that you are Peter, and on this rock I will build my church, and the gates of Hades will not overcome it."

Matthew 16:15–18

"My soul is overwhelmed with sorrow to the point of death," he said to them. "Stay here and keep watch." Going a little farther, he fell to the ground and prayed that if possible the hour might pass from him. "Abba, Father," he said, "everything is possible for you. Take this cup from me. Yet not what I will, but what you will." Then he returned to his disciples and found them sleeping. "Simon," he said to Peter, "are you asleep? Could you not keep watch for one hour? Watch and pray so that you will not fall into temptation. The spirit is willing, but the body is weak."

Mark 14:34–38

The only time Luke uses the "Simon Peter" combination is in chapter 5, verse 8, of his gospel; every other time he refers to this apostle as Simon *or* Peter. What's the significance of Luke's unique strategy? Unable to catch any fish all night, Peter, the seasoned fisherman, let discouragement walk right in. Jesus spoke up, offering some fishing advice.

When he had finished speaking, he said to Simon, "Put out into deep water, and let down the nets for a catch." Simon answered,

> *"Master, we've worked hard all night and haven't caught anything. But because you say so, I will let down the nets."*
>
> Luke 5:4-5

Still, no matter how much experience you have, how can you argue with the one who created the fish?

> *When they had done so, they caught such a large number of fish that their nets began to break. So they signaled their partners in the other boat to come and help them, and they came and filled both boats so full that they began to sink.*
>
> Luke 5:6–7

Although illogical, Jesus' advice worked, and Simon's lack of faith was exposed—not an unfamiliar occurrence. (Remember the whole walking-on-water and then falling-in-water scenario? Jesus renamed him Peter—"the Rock." Instead of acting like one, Peter sank like one.)

This primary apostle was susceptible to the dualism of fear and faith that plagued his heart, and Luke lets us into this battle when he refers to him by both names:

> *When Simon Peter saw this, he fell at Jesus' knees and said, "Go away from me, Lord; I am a sinful man!" For he and all his companions were astonished at the catch of fish they had taken, and so were James and John, the sons of Zebedee, Simon's partners. Then Jesus said to Simon, "Don't be afraid; from now on you will catch men."*
>
> Luke 5:8–10

Sometimes Peter operated out of fear. The writer Luke pulled back the covers on this behavior when referring to Peter exclusively by his old name, Simon. In the upper room, on the cusp of Jesus' darkest hour, Peter, along with the other

ADDITIONAL INSIGHT ON SECRET NAMES

disciples, was fighting about (of all things) which disciple was the greatest.

Rather than referring to Peter as "the Rock," Jesus addressed him by his old name and lovingly communicated his commitment to pray for him in his darkest hour—as if to say, "OK, Simon, you think you're great (hence the recent argument with the other disciples), but you're actually about to embody incredible weakness."

> *"Simon, Simon, Satan has asked to sift you as wheat. But I have prayed for you, Simon, that your faith may not fail. And when you have turned back, strengthen your brothers."*
>
> Luke 22:31–32

By using Simon's Birth Name, Jesus tenderly tried to prepare Peter for the trial about to knock on his door. By praying for Peter, Jesus hoped Peter would recognize his need for God's strength. Instead, Peter's reply indicated he thought he was strong enough without God.

Rather than humbly accepting this prayer support from the Son of God, Simon shrugged it off, inaccurately communicating his unfaltering resolve to be great by acting like the dependable "rock" his new name suggests. He conveyed this commitment with an air of arrogance:

> *But he replied, "Lord, I am ready to go with you to prison and to death."*
>
> Luke 22:33

Jesus, picking up on Simon's strong show, followed suit by addressing him with his new name, Peter. It's as if Jesus is saying to Simon, "OK, 'Rock,' I'll interact with you on this level. You think you're immune to fear? In reality, you're just hours away from denying that you even know me."

Jesus answered, "I tell you, Peter, before the rooster crows today, you will deny three times that you know me."

Luke 22:34

After his death and resurrection, Jesus—known for his patience—circles back to reinstate Peter—known for his denial. Scholars key in on the fact that Jesus asked Peter *three times* if he loved him—obviously the same number of times that Peter denied Jesus. Rather than referring to his friend by his new name, Peter, Jesus again calls him by his old name, Simon.

> *When they had finished eating, Jesus said to Simon Peter, "Simon son of John, do you truly love me more than these?"*
>
> *"Yes, Lord," he said, "you know that I love you."*
>
> *Jesus said, "Feed my lambs."*
>
> *Again Jesus said, "Simon son of John, do you truly love me?"*
>
> *He answered, "Yes, Lord, you know that I love you."*
>
> *Jesus said, "Take care of my sheep."*
>
> *The third time he said to him, "Simon son of John, do you love me?"*
>
> *Peter was hurt because Jesus asked him the third time, "Do you love me?" He said, "Lord, you know all things; you know that I love you."*
>
> *Jesus said, "Feed my sheep."*

John 21:15–17

Ever the believer, Jesus commissioned Peter with the incredibly important task of feeding his sheep. He thought of Peter still worthy if he could remain teachable and moldable. About to split and shoot back up to heaven, Jesus took the time to charge Peter with a tremendous opportunity, trusting him despite his recent failures. Jesus knew his friend's success was intrinsically tied to his ability to act like Peter—a man of faith. For this reason, he reminds him of his Birth Name, Simon—a man of fear.

Jesus never wanted Peter to forget his Birth Name. Remembering it produced meekness and gratitude. Meekness, because Peter knew his Secret Name was more about God than it was about him. Gratitude, because Peter knew what he'd been saved from.

Thankfully for us, Peter accepted Jesus' charge and dedicated his life to preach the gospel of salvation and Secret Names until he drew his last breath on this earth.

Appendix 2
The ABCs of Your Identity

The Bible reveals a treasure trove of riches regarding your new identity. These become true for you once you choose to be in relationship with God through Jesus Christ's finished work on the cross. Enjoy these ABCs of your Identity. Start spending them now, this side of eternity. (The best news is they never run out.)

My Identity—Who I am . . .	
Accepted in the beloved	Ephesians 1:6
Bought with a price	1 Corinthians 6:20
Crucified with Christ	Galatians 2:20
Dwelt by the Holy Spirit	1 Corinthians 3:16
Enslaved to God	Romans 6:22
Freed from slavery to sin	Romans 6:18
God's child	Romans 8:14
Heir of God's riches	Galatians 4:6–7
In him complete	Colossians 2:10
Jesus' chosen inheritance	Ephesians 1:4

My Identity—Who I am . . .	
Kingly priest	1 Peter 2:9
Light of the world	Matthew 5:14
Mastered no longer by sin	Romans 6:14
New creation	2 Corinthians 5:14
One spirit with the Lord	1 Corinthians 6:17
Perfect in Christ	Hebrews 10:14
Quieted in who God is	Psalm 46:10
Raised up with him	Ephesians 2:5–6
Seated in heavenly places	Ephesians 2:5–6
Transformed into Christ's image	2 Corinthians 3:18
United to the Lord	1 Corinthians 6:17
Victorious through my Lord	1 Corinthians 15:57
Wonderfully made	Psalm 139:14
Xristos' workmanship	Ephesians 2:10
Yoked with righteousness	2 Corinthians 6:14
Zealous of good works	Titus 2:14

APPENDIX 3
DISCUSSION POINTS

INTRODUCTION: THE GENTLE WHISPER

1. When is the last time you wondered who you really are?
2. Are you completely secure in understanding who you are? Why or why not?
3. Please explain what currently shapes your identity.
4. Are you fully resolved concerning certain monumental issues, like discerning your purpose, calling, and lot in this life?
5. What fears do you have related to exploring the Name Game?

CHAPTER 1: A WORLD WITHOUT NAMES

1. What's the meaning of your Birth Name? If you don't know, please research it.
2. What are some of the Given Names people have granted you?

3. Who gave you these names and why? How did/does hearing these names make you feel?

4. How have you tried to hide from these name(s)?

5. Do you believe you've been created for more than your life presently reflects? If not, why not? If so, do you have any indication what this destiny might be?

Chapter 2: The Statue Maker

1. What does the story of the Statue Maker reveal about God's nature?

2. How does your life reflect that you're frozen? How does your life reflect that you're free?

3. Which path have you spent the most time on—the path of religion or rebellion? What events led to your choice?

4. Have you ever felt as if God is uninterested in you or the details of your life? What led to this type of thinking?

5. How have you tried to create a new name for yourself? Has it worked? If not, why not?

Chapter 3: The Name Game

1. How have you let what you do overshadow who you are?

2. Is your identity healthy or unhealthy? Please explain your answer.

3. If what you DO was stripped from your life, how would your life change? How would your self-esteem change?

4. Describe the best period of your life. What made it special?

DISCUSSION POINTS

5. What was your relationship with others during this period? Describe your relationship with God during this period.

CHAPTER 4: PUPPETS AND PAWNS

1. How have you been used by someone within the Name Game? How did you feel?

2. How have you used someone within the Name Game? How did you feel?

3. Have you worked through your wounds, or are you still in the process of healing? If you've been healed, what contributed to this healing? If you're still in process, what action steps do you need to take?

4. Describe your relationship or lack of relationship with your parents. What emotions do you feel concerning them? Why?

5. What emotions do you feel concerning God? Why?

CHAPTER 5: IMPOSTER SYNDROME

1. Have you ever felt like an imposter? If so, please describe the details (when, where, why).

2. Assess the "condition of your soul."

3. On a scale of 1 to 10 (1 = poor / 10 = exceptional), how authentic are you? Where is it most difficult for you to be real? Why is it difficult?

4. What things would have to change in order for you to be real in those places?

5. Have you ever received a blessing from someone? How did it make you feel? Have you ever given someone a blessing? How did they respond?

Chapter 6: Till We Have Names

1. How have you contributed to someone else's namelessness (for example, when referring to others as *those people, teenagers today* . . .)?
2. How do you think a nameless person feels? Why?
3. What type of culture is created when people are stripped of their names?
4. How has the Enemy tried to use you within the Name Game?
5. In reference to Pascal's quote, are you able to sit quietly in a room by yourself? Why or why not?

Chapter 7: Three Heartbreaks

1. Which do you value most: your sense of identity, acceptance, or independence? Why?
2. Why do you think God often allows us to reach rock bottom before allowing us to discover our Secret Name?
3. If you've been given a peek at your Secret Name, what did you see?
4. In life, what type of experiences have you memorialized? Why were those experiences worth memorializing?
5. Please describe the time you felt farthest from God.

DISCUSSION POINTS

CHAPTER 8: GRACE INTERRUPTED

1. What lies do you swallow even though you know they're not rooted in truth? Why?

2. Do you like to be alone? If so, why? If so, when? If so, where? If you don't like to be alone, why not?

3. Describe your most beautiful memory of nature.

4. Has God ever spoken to you? What did he say? If not, why do you think this is?

5. What promises have you ever made to God? Why? What promises has he made to you?

CHAPTER 9: MIRRORS TELL HALF-TRUTHS

1. Who has been a truth teller for you? Who is a truth teller to you now?

2. How did you respond when they spoke into your life?

3. Please explain a time when someone else deceived you?

4. Have you ever worked through the pain? If not, what would it take for you to experience healing?

5. At this point in the story, is your Secret Name becoming any clearer? If not, how does that make you feel?

CHAPTER 10: PACKING YOUR SUITCASE

1. Describe a time when God rescued you from a less than ideal scenario.

2. Describe a time when you prayed fervently.

3. Did God answer your prayers the way you wanted? If so, how? If not, why not?
4. Describe a time when you received an unexpected gift.
5. How did receiving that gift encourage you?

Chapter 11: In the Camp of Angels

1. Describe a time when you tried to get yourself out of a jam. Did it work? If not, why not?
2. When have you allowed fear to paralyze you?
3. Are you angry at God for the pain he has allowed in your life? In your past, have you ever been angry at God?
4. Have you ever experienced the "dark night of the soul"? How do you know?
5. What did you learn about God as a result?

Chapter 12: Pushing Through the Past

1. Describe a time when someone mentored you. How did it help? How did it hurt?
2. Please describe a time when you withdrew from a relationship. Why did you pull back?
3. Has there ever been a period of your life when you experienced sleeplessness? If so, what were the details?
4. Have you ever had a relationship form unexpectedly?
5. Please share about a time when you were depressed. What caused it and did you break free from it? If so, how?

Discussion Points

Chapter 13: The Divine Wound

1. Describe a time when you wrestled God. What did you learn from your experience?
2. How well do you do at expressing emotions? What contributes to your ability or inability?
3. Share the details surrounding a divine wound that took place in your life.
4. When in pain, what coping mechanisms do you employ?
5. If you've received a divine wound, how do you now walk with a limp? What does this limp communicate about your relationship or lack of relationship with God?

Chapter 14: The White Stone

1. Are you still trying to hide behind your Given Names? Are you ready to receive your Secret Name?
2. If you're ready, what led you to this point? If you're not ready, what's stopping you?
3. Imagine yourself standing before God. Do you see yourself as guilty or innocent? What thoughts contributed to your answer?
4. Imagine yourself standing before God. What name does he whisper when speaking to you?
5. If you're a follower of Jesus, is it hard for you to think of yourself as a new creation? Why or why not?

Chapter 15: Sacred Spaces

1. If you've learned your Secret Name, how did you discover it?

2. If you don't know your Secret Name, what steps will you take to learn it? Will you exercise importunity in this process?

3. Please describe one of your Sacred Spaces.

4. What is one of your Secret Names for God? Why?

5. Give three practical ways you can strengthen your Secret Name.

Appendix 4
Notes

Chapter 1: A World without Names

1. A quick glance in the first two chapters of Genesis seems to produce one single occurrence of a human name prior to the time of sin. However, a closer look reveals that this reference to Adam found only in Genesis 2:20 isn't the personal name it initially seems to be.

    The Hebrew word for Adam, *ādām*, literally means "man" or "mankind." This Hebrew word is the exact same word found in Genesis 2:19, translated there as "man" and not "Adam," as in verse 20. "Adam" and "man" are used interchangeably. Therefore, it's consistent that, prior to sin, humans were named only for what they were (gender and species = male/female and man/woman), not who they were (personal names = Adam/Eve).

2. James M. Freeman, *Manners and Customs of the Bible* (Plainfield, N.J.: Logos International, 1972), 38.

3. The promised seed never came through Cain's line, but rather through Seth's line. Seth was the third son of Adam and Eve.

4. "You are just a vapor that appears for a little while and then vanishes" (James 4:14 NASB).

5. Warren W. Wiersbe, "Gen. 4:1," *Wiersbe's Expository Outlines on the Old Testament* (Wheaton, Ill.: Victor, 1993).

6. This fulfillment took place millennia later in the person of Jesus Christ, crucified upon a cruel cross.

7. For more information on Given Names, please see *www.YourSecretName.com*

CHAPTER 2: THE STATUE MAKER

1. For more on this topic, see John Eldredge, *Wild at Heart: Discovering the Secret of a Man's Soul* (Nashville: Nelson, 2001).

2. Such people embody Ferdinand Foch's quote: "The most powerful weapon on earth is the human soul on fire." Spoken September 1914 during the First Battle of the Marne in World War I and quoted in Harold Whittle Blakely, *The 32nd Infantry Division in World War II* (1956), 3.

CHAPTER 4: PUPPETS AND PAWNS

1. Greg Johnson, "Father who gave son steroids: I hurt my family," *Grand Rapids Press*, January 30, 2008, Mlive: http://blog.mlive.com/grpress/2008/01/convicted_father_son_appear_on.html (August 9, 2008).

2. Elaine Silvestrini, "Dad Who Gave Son Steroids Is Given 6-Year Prison Term," January 7, 2008, *Tampa Tribune*: www2.tbo.com/content/2008/jan/07/dad-who-gave-son-steroids-given-6-year-prison-term (August 9, 2008).

3. M. G. Easton, *Easton's Bible Dictionary* (Oak Harbor, Wash.: Logos Research Systems, 1996).

4. The concept of firstborn resonated deeply with most ancient Near East cultures. However, the messianic overtones contained in the Scriptures made it reverberate uniquely in the ears of the Jewish people (Zechariah 12:10). Ever since Adam and Eve's fall in the garden, the promised people anxiously awaited the promised "firstborn" redeemer, who would deliver them and grant them a double portion of inheritance (Isaiah 61:7). Walter A.

NOTES

Elwell, Philip Wesley Comfort, *Tyndale Bible Dictionary*, Tyndale Reference Library (Wheaton, Ill.: Tyndale, 2001), 485.

5. These blessings weren't confined to Jews only. The significance of the firstborn spread from Israel and the Old Testament era into the church and the New Testament era. Followers of Jesus who recognized him as the Messiah also recognized his preeminence. He is called "the firstborn among many brothers" (Romans 8:29) and "the head of the body, the church; he is the beginning and the firstborn from among the dead, so that in everything he might have the supremacy" (Colossians 1:18).

CHAPTER 5: IMPOSTER SYNDROME

1. Traditionally the eldest son received the blessing.

CHAPTER 6: TILL WE HAVE NAMES

1. Daniel Lapin, "Names Matter," October 30, 2008, *Thought Tools*, 44, first day of Cheshvan, 5769 Issue 44, *hwww.rabbidaniellapin.com/thoughttools/ThoughtToolsIssue44NamesMatter.pdf* (October 30, 2008).

2. Blaise Pascal, *Pensées*, trans. W. F. Trotter (1944), no. 139.

CHAPTER 8: GRACE INTERRUPTED

1. Jeremiah 29:12
2. Jeremiah 29:13
3. Jeremiah 29:14
4. Jeremiah 29:14

Chapter 13: The Divine Wound

1. Genesis 18:17–33; Exodus 32:24–30; Matthew 26:37–46.
2. Bill Patterson, *Big Bottom Church* (Nashville: CrossBooks, 2010), 159.
3. Psalm 23.
4. Importunity accurately describes the widow in Luke 18. The Bible says that Jesus taught this parable in order to "show them that they should always pray and not give up" (v. 1).

Chapter 14: The White Stone

1. "Blackball," *Merriam-Webster's Collegiate Dictionary*, 11th ed. (Springfield, Mass.: Merriam-Webster, 2003).

Chapter 15: Sacred Spaces

1. I talk about this tendency in much more detail in "Extras for Pastors, Teachers, Leaders, and Counselors," page 179.

ACKNOWLEDGMENTS

To my family: Kelly, Keegan, Isabel, and Addison. Life wouldn't make sense without you. You keep me ignited.

To my business partner, David Branderhorst, and our current team that's growing every day: Emily Myers, Abigail Young, Nanette O'Neal, Erica McCuen, Tanisha Williams, Gennean Woodall, Daphne Smith, Debra Hayes, Lisa Moser, Niccie Kliegl, Matthew Waite, Chris O'Byrne, and Brenda and Tim Dunagan. Business wouldn't work without you. You keep the tribe and me ablaze.

ABOUT THE AUTHOR

KARY OBERBRUNNER is igniting souls. Through his writing, speaking, and coaching, he helps individuals and organizations clarify who they are, why they're here, and where they should invest their time and energy.

Kary struggled to find his distinct voice and passion. As a young man, he suffered from severe stuttering, depression, and self-injury. Today a transformed man, Kary equips people to experience unhackability in work and life and share their message with the world. In the past twenty years, he's ignited over one million people with his content. He lives in Ohio with his wife, Kelly, and three kids.

ABOUT THE PUBLISHER

Kary Oberbrunner and David Branderhorst created Author Academy Elite in 2014 rather by accident. Their clients kept asking for a program to help them write, publish, and market their books the right way.

After months of resisting, they shared a new publishing paradigm one evening in March on a private call. They had nothing built and knew it would take six months to implement that idea and create a premium experience.

Regardless of the unknowns, twenty-five aspiring authors jumped in immediately, and Author Academy Elite was born. Today, Author Academy Elite attracts hundreds of quality authors who share a mutual commitment to create vibrant businesses around their books.

AUTHOR ACADEMY elite

AuthorAcademyElite.com

ABOUT IGNITING SOULS

ignitingsouls

We are a tribe. We view and do life differently. We believe this:

- Clarity attracts. Confusion repels.
- There are two types of people in the world: those that let the world happen to them and those that happen to the world. Although this difference is subtle, it makes all the difference.
- The glory of God is a person fully alive.
- We were created to show up filled up.
- The most powerful weapon on earth is the human soul on fire.

- The most damaging thing in the life of a child is the unlived life of a parent.
- Souls on fire know WHO they are (identity), WHY they're here (purpose), and WHERE they're going (direction).

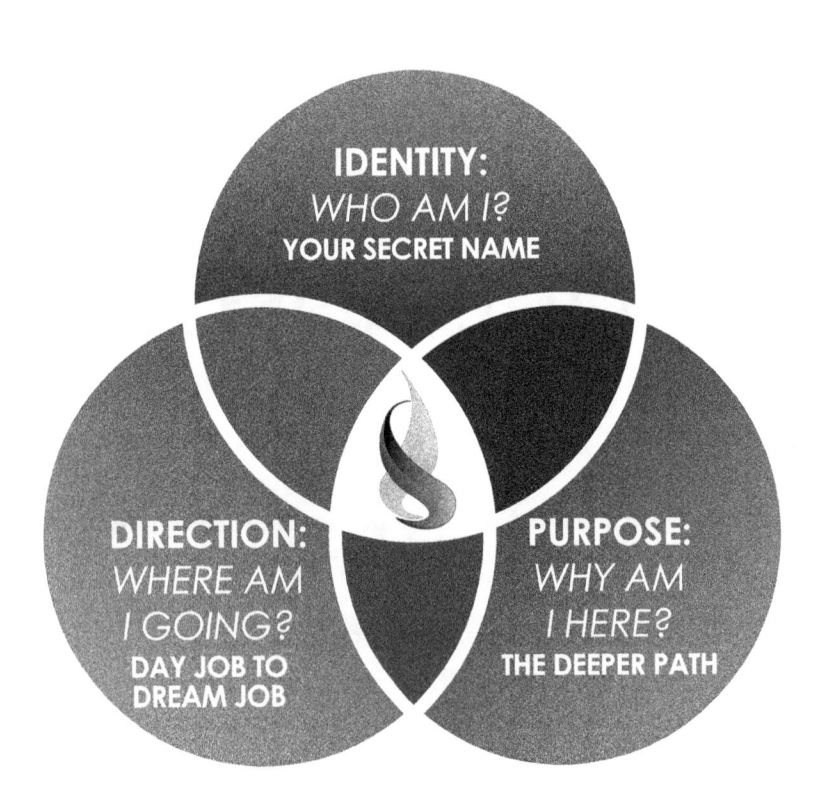

IDENTITY:
WHO AM I?
YOUR SECRET NAME

DIRECTION:
WHERE AM I GOING?
DAY JOB TO DREAM JOB

PURPOSE:
WHY AM I HERE?
THE DEEPER PATH

Your Next Steps with *Your Secret Name*

✓ **TAKE THE FREE ASSESSMENT:**
Get your Unique Score

✓ **EXPERIENCE KARY'S FREE MASTER CLASS:**
Reset your Self-Image Set Point

✓ **DO YOUR SECRET NAME 5-WEEK JOURNEY:**
Discover Your Secret Name

✓ **JOIN YOUR SECRET NAME TEAM:**
Become a Certified Coach | Speaker | Trainer

YourSecretName.com

Don't live another day without knowing your purpose.

DeeperPathBook.com

Go as you please, earn as you wish, and live as you like.

Start living your dream job today!

DayJobtoDreamJob.com

Everything can be hacked, even the truth.

ELIXIR PROJECT

KARY OBERBRUNNER

ElixirProjectBook.com

START YOUR DAY WITH A SPARK.

ignitingsouls
DAILY SHOW

WITH KARY OBERBRUNNER

Want to begin your day the right way?
Check out the Igniting Souls Daily Show.
Each brief episode provides practical wisdom for life and business.
Get your daily dose of inspiration and start your day with a Spark.

Listen on **Apple Podcasts**

Listen on Google **Play Music**

Watch us on **YouTube**

SUBSCRIBE TODAY!

CPSIA information can be obtained
at www.ICGtesting.com
Printed in the USA
FFHW01n0452021018